The Best is Yet to Come

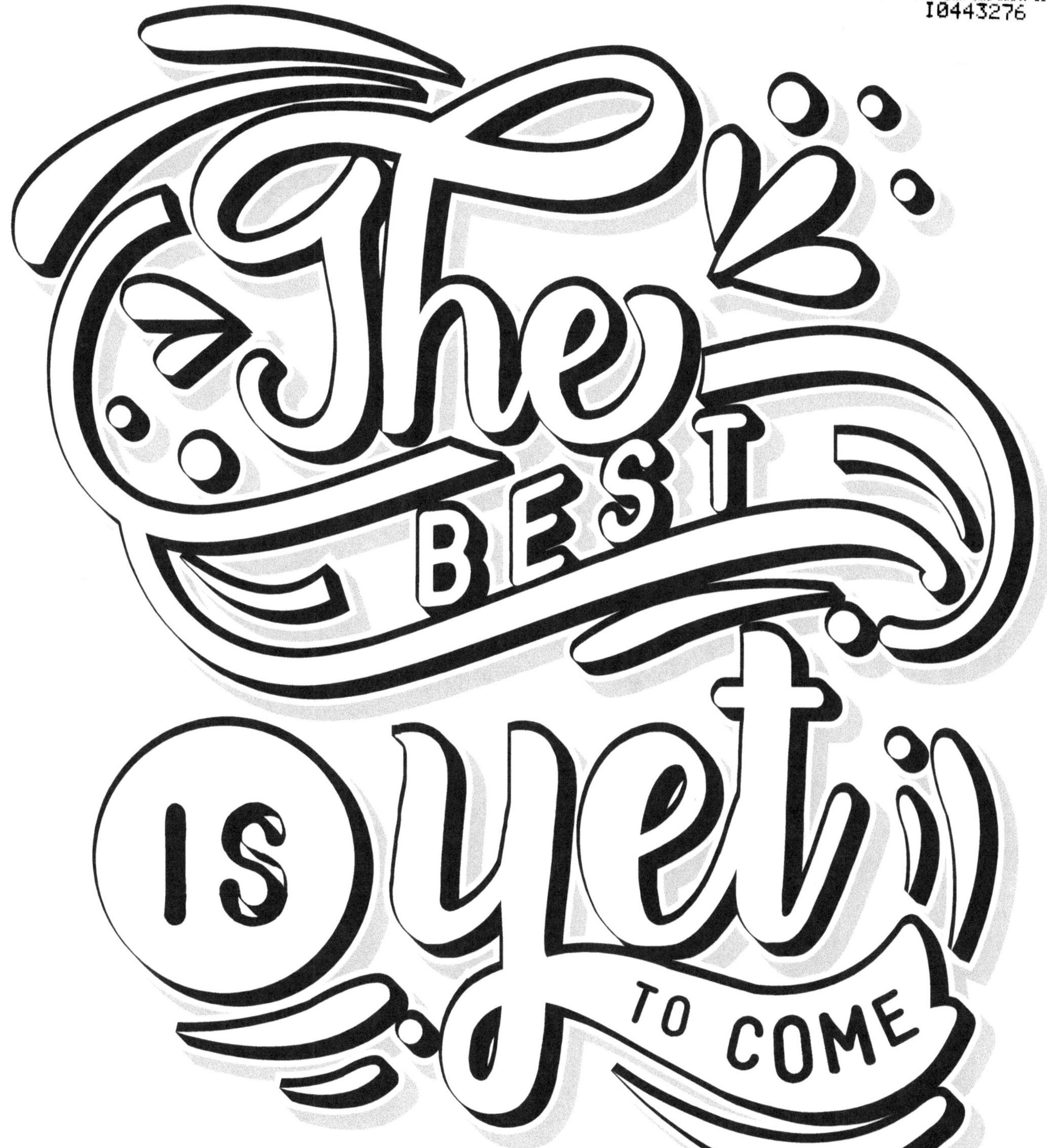

35 motivational quotes to color

© 2020 SHECOLORS
ALL RIGHTS RESERVED

This page left intentionally blank.

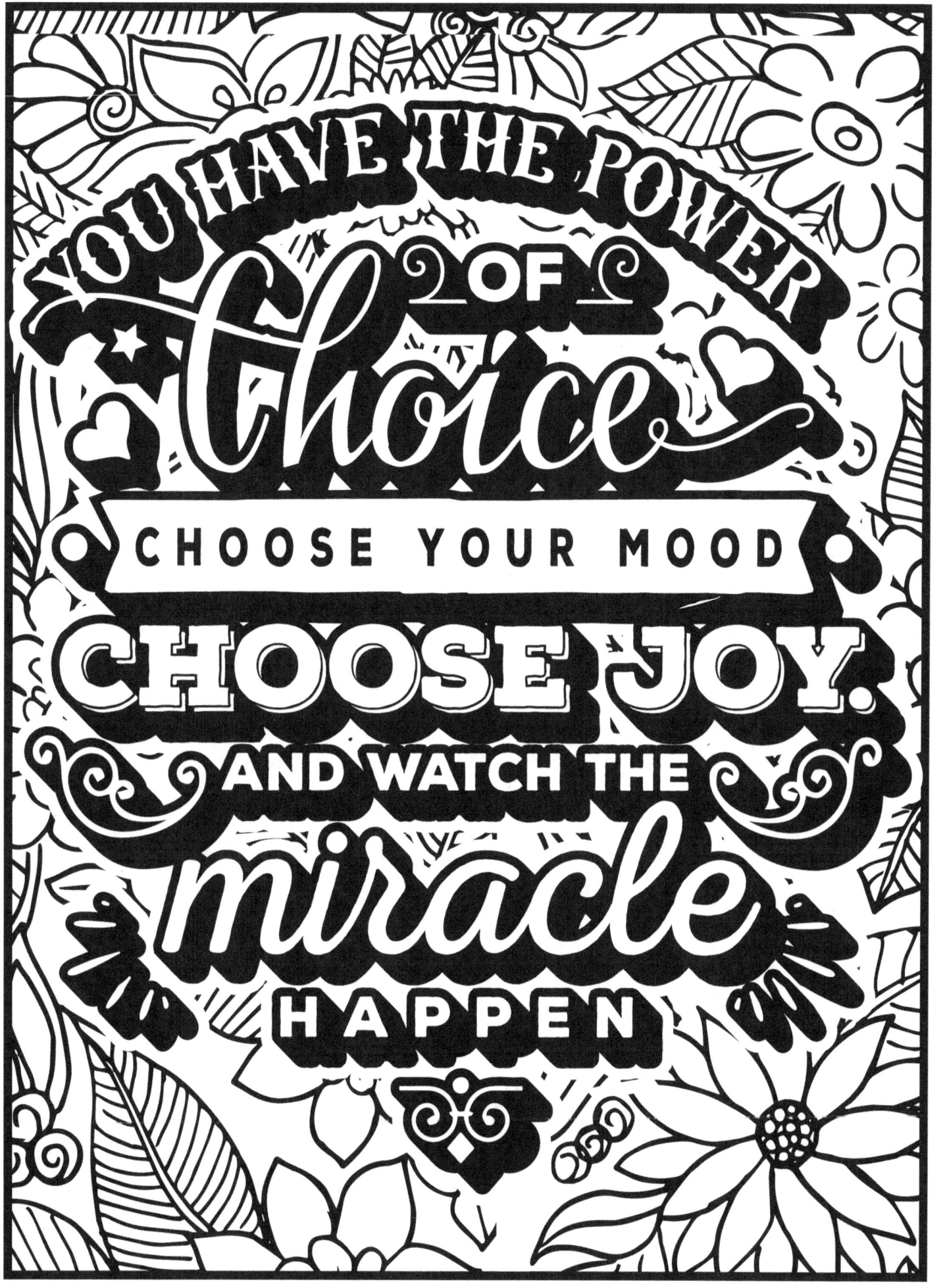

This page left intentionally blank.

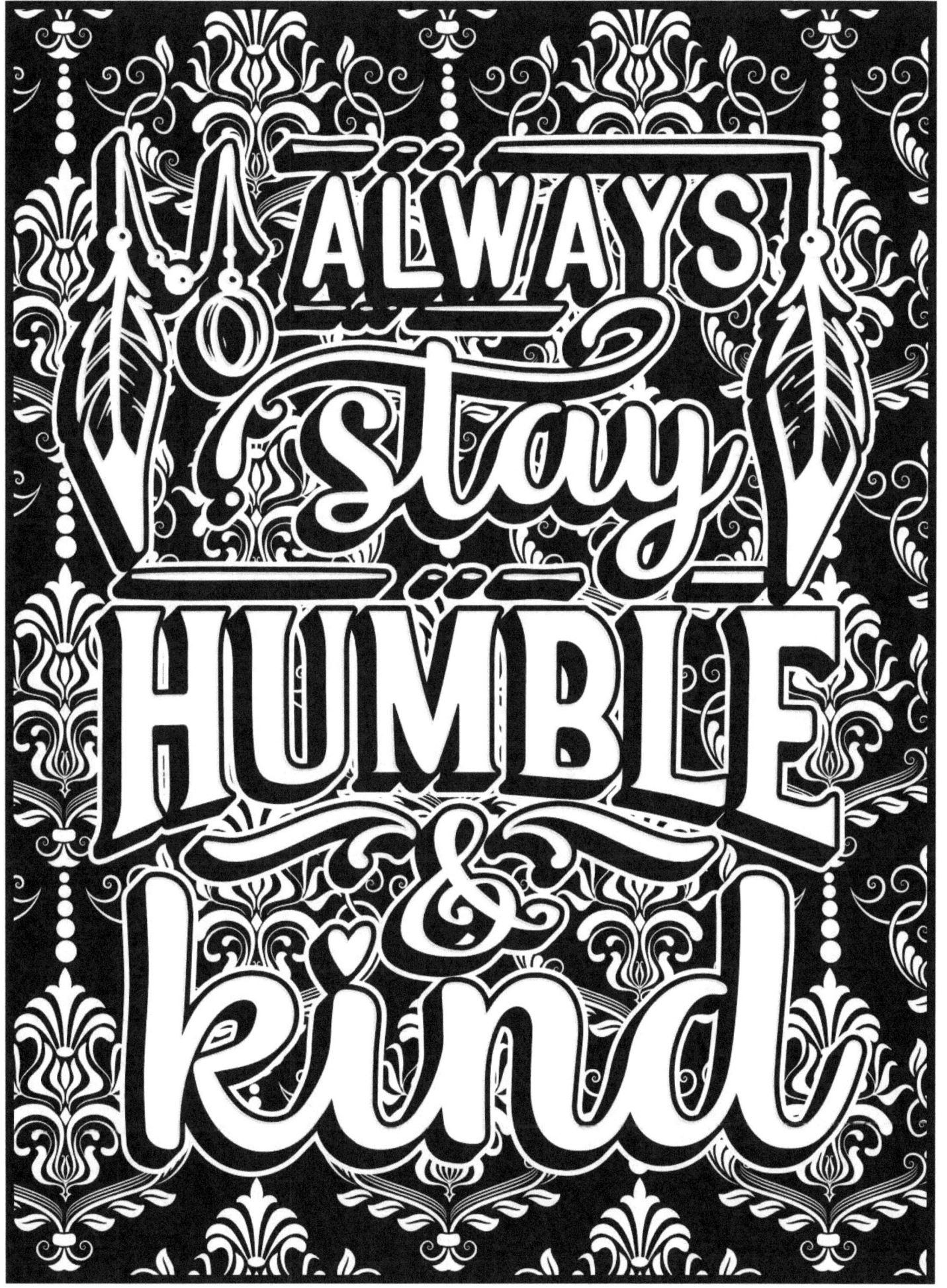

This page left intentionally blank.

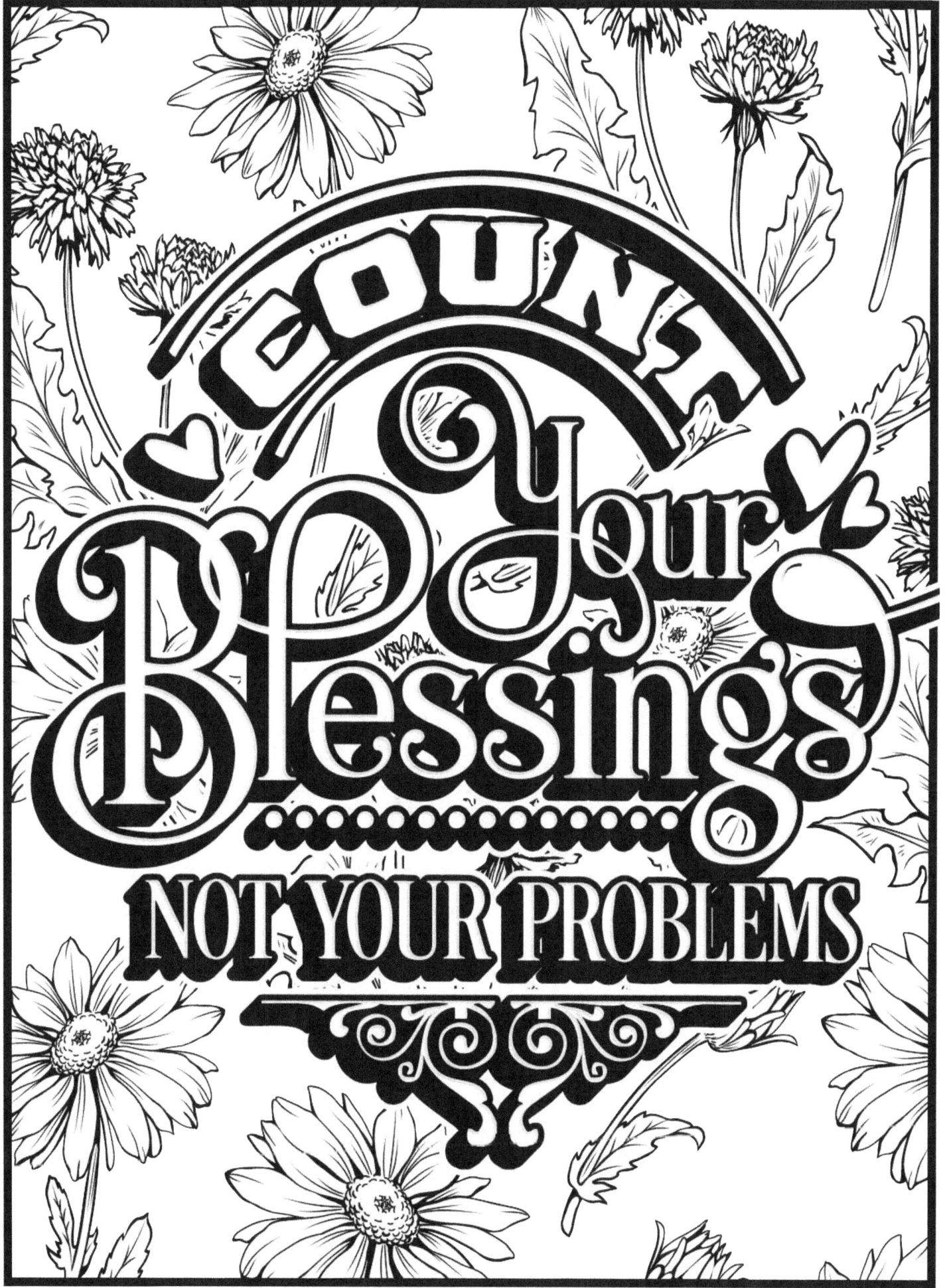

This page left intentionally blank.

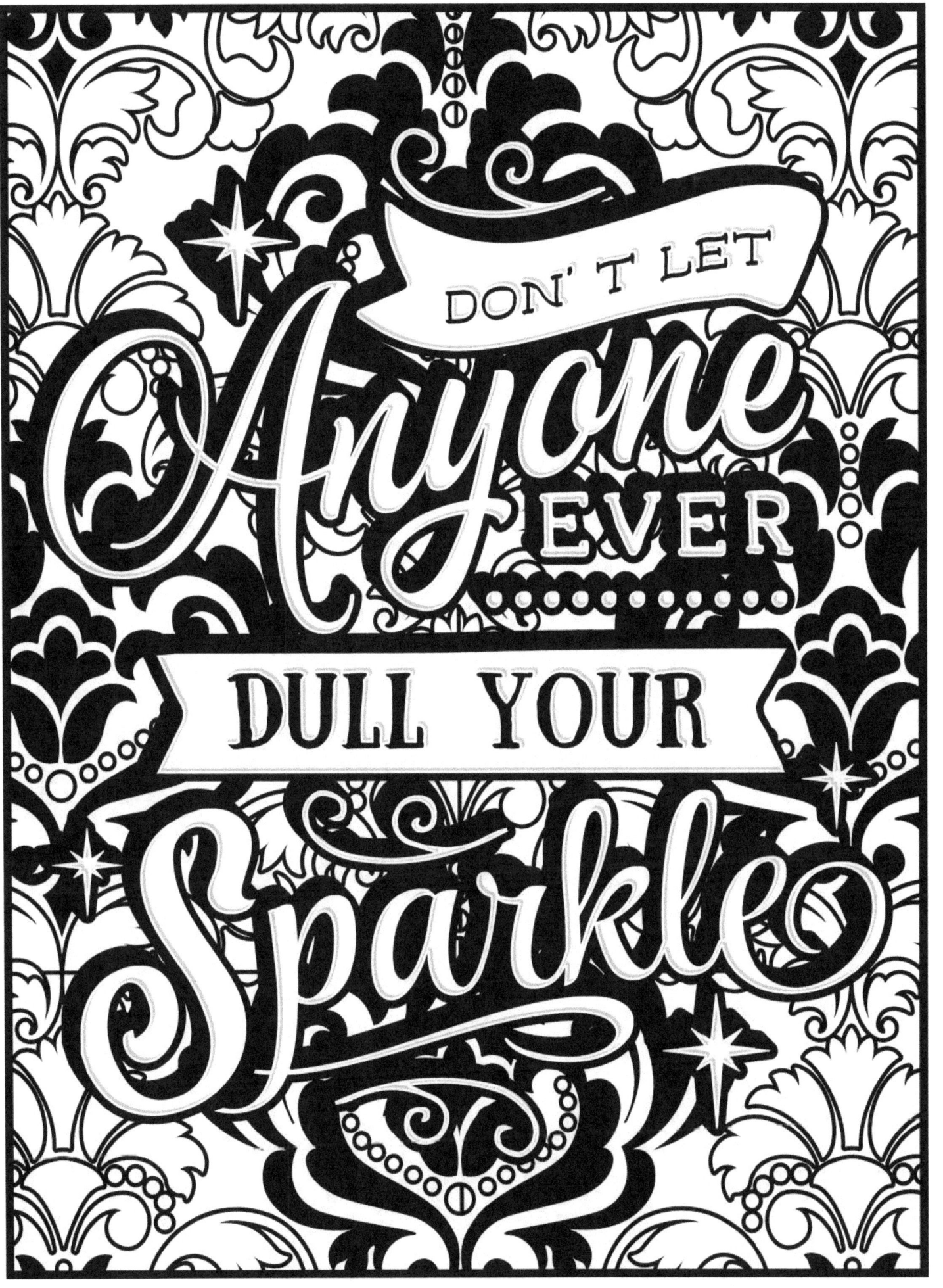

This page left intentionally blank.

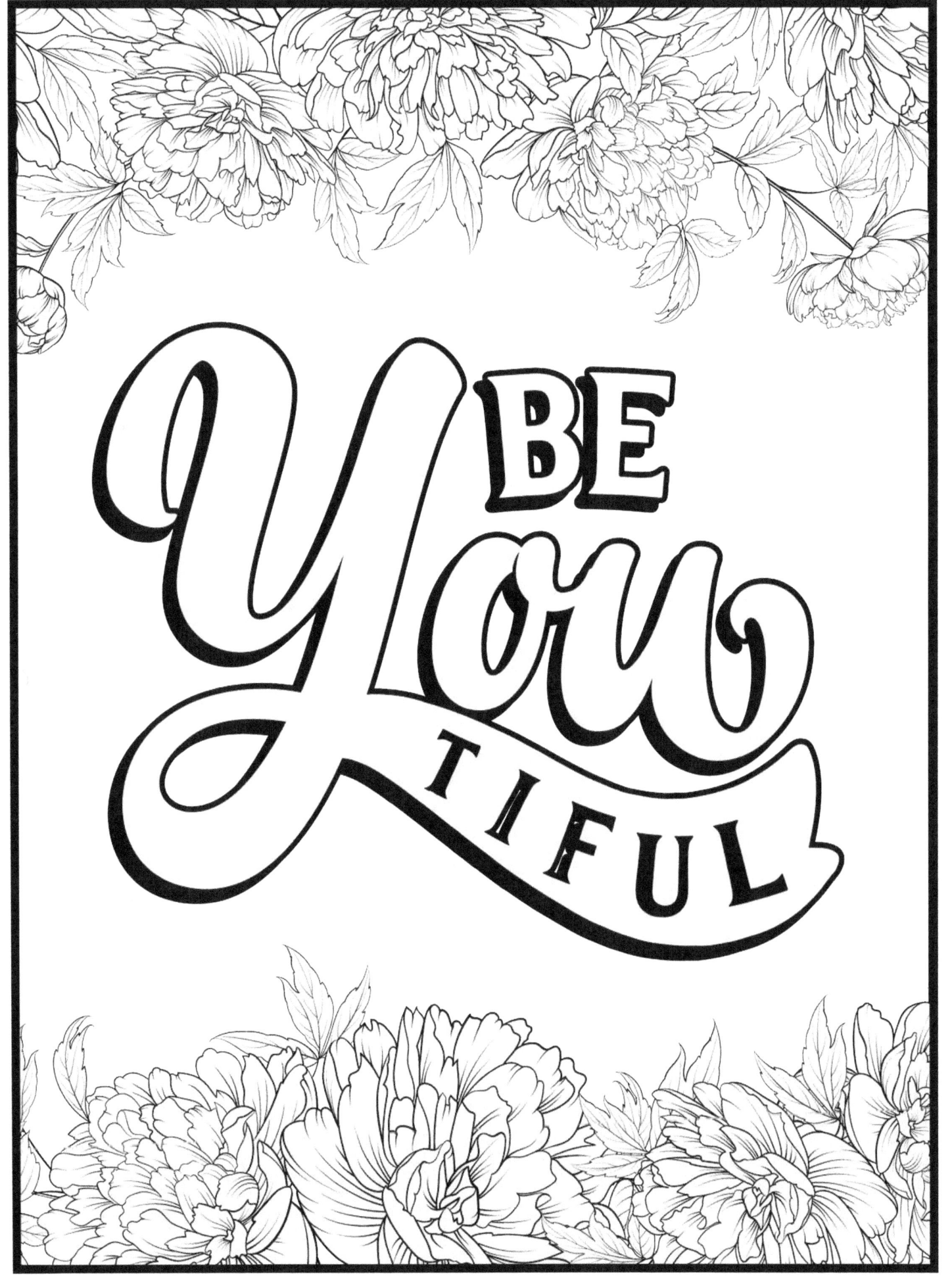

This page left intentionally blank.

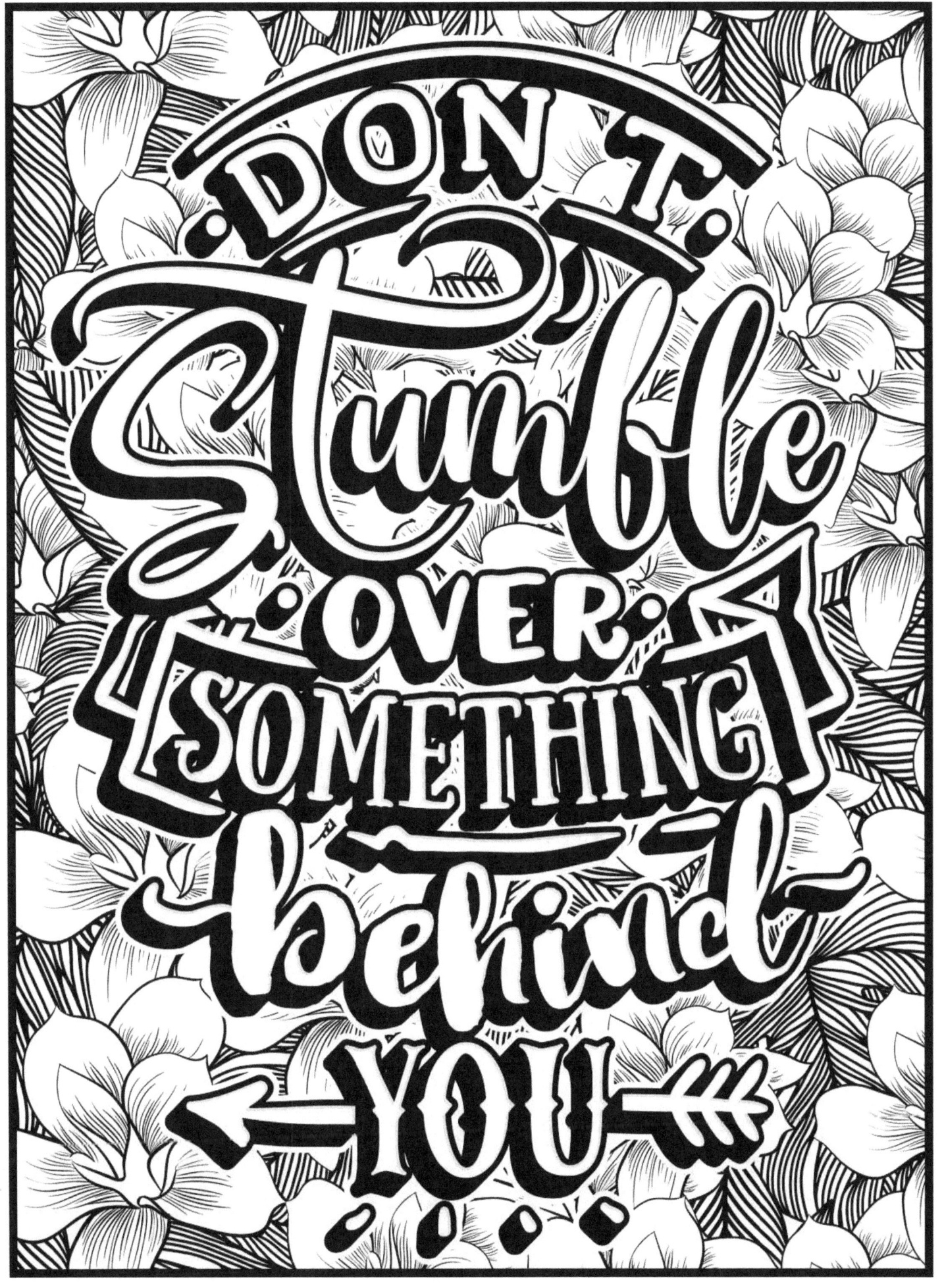

This page left intentionally blank.

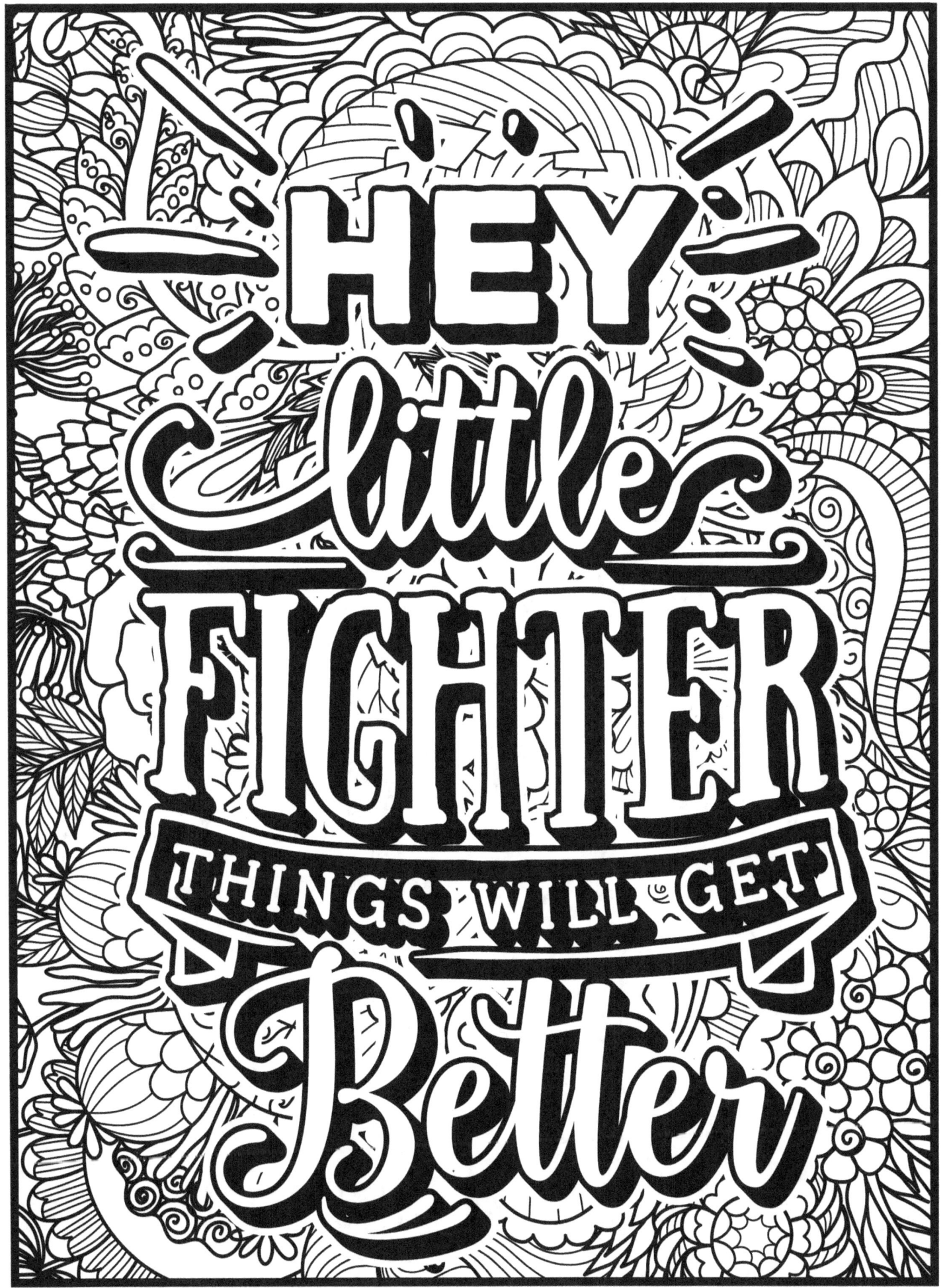

This page left intentionally blank.

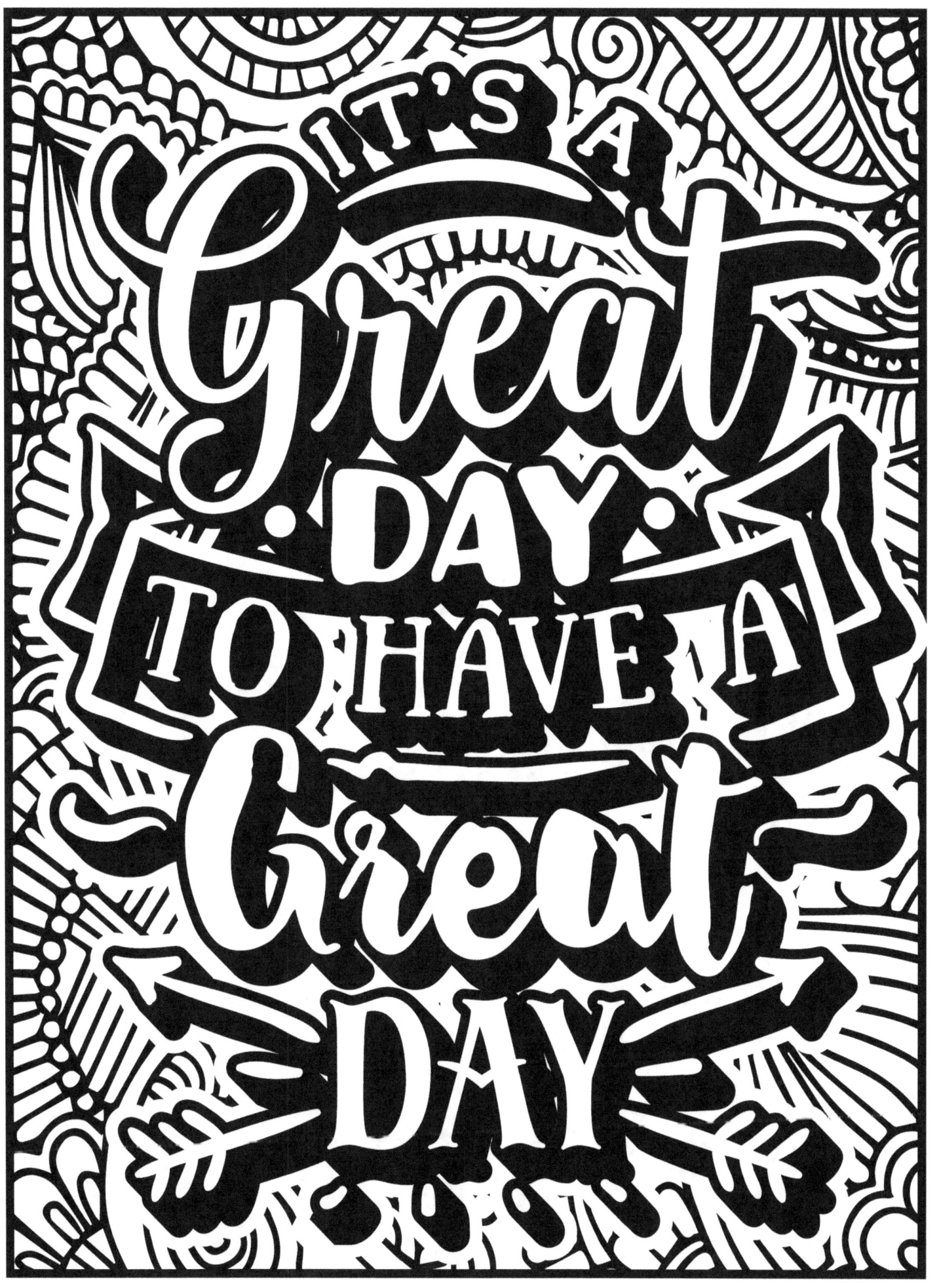

This page left intentionally blank.

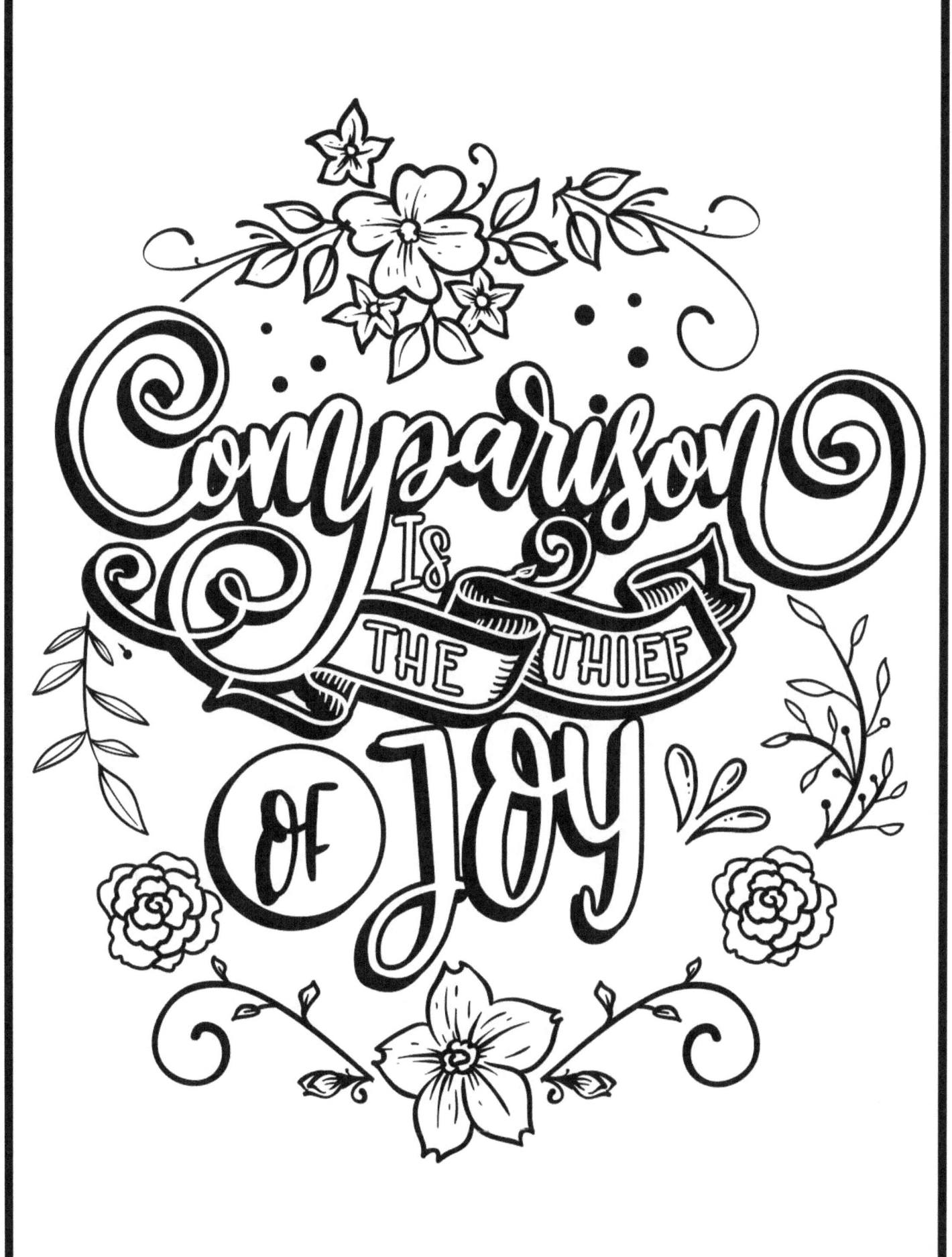

This page left intentionally blank.

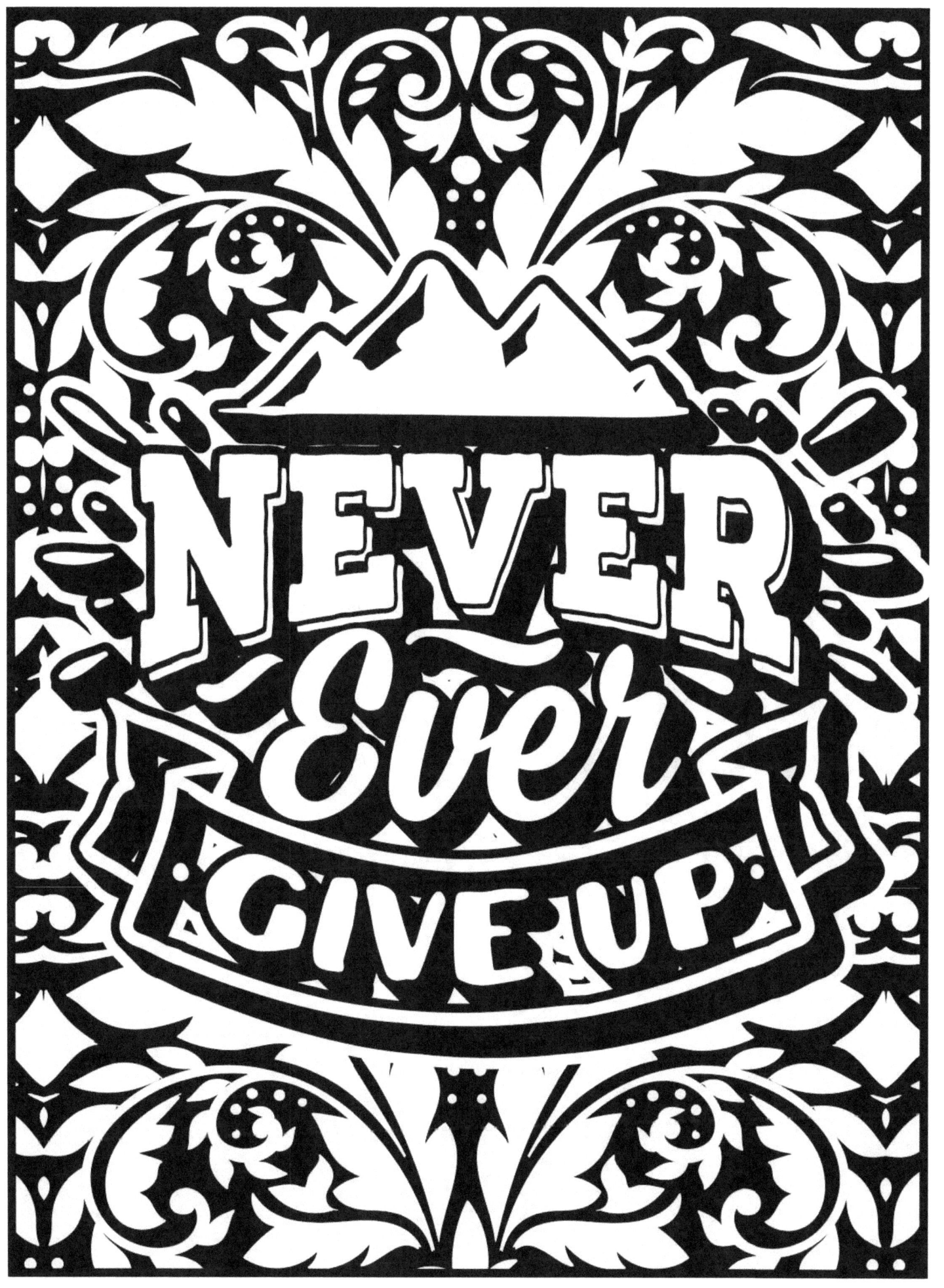

This page left intentionally blank.

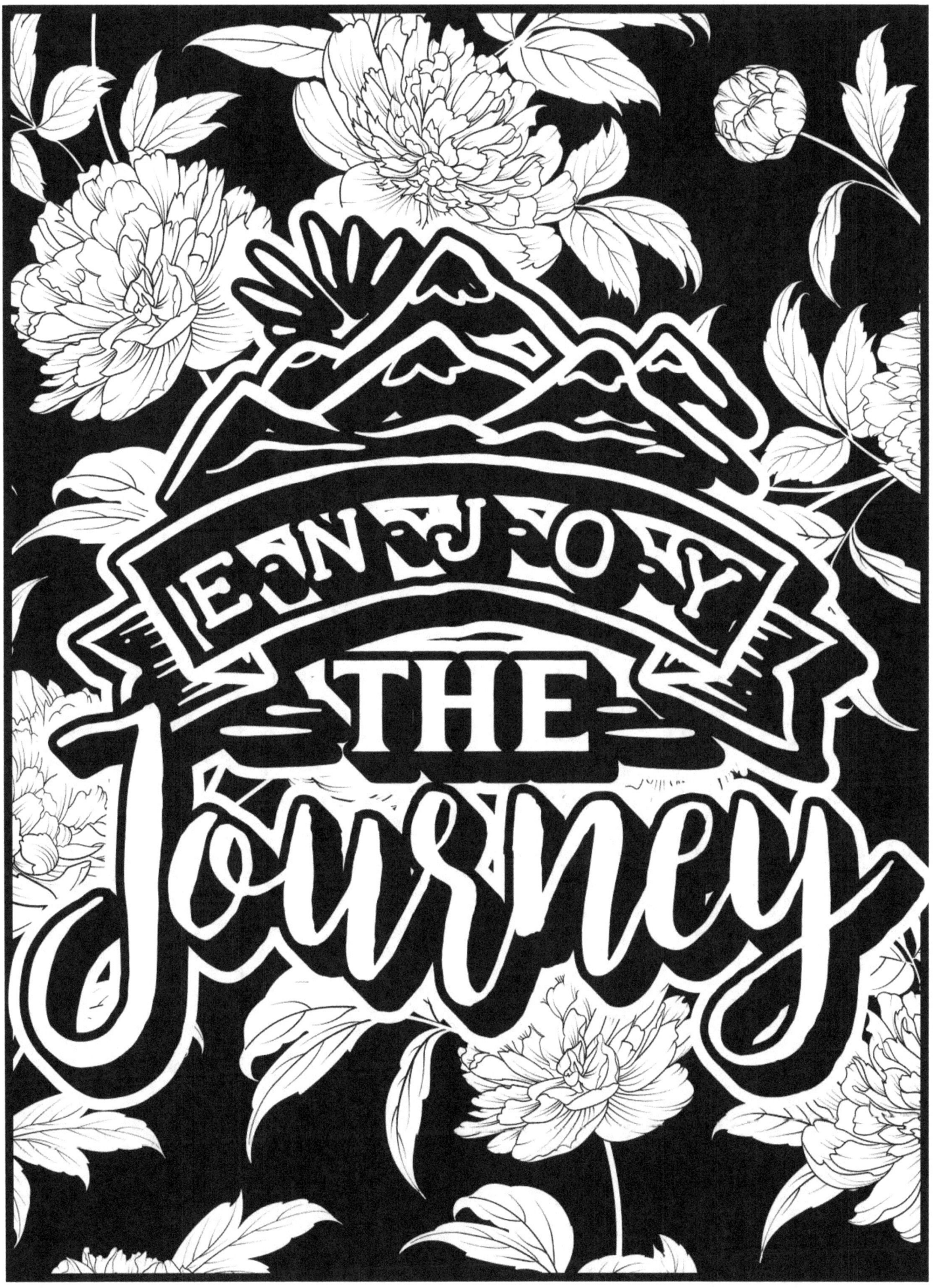

This page left intentionally blank.

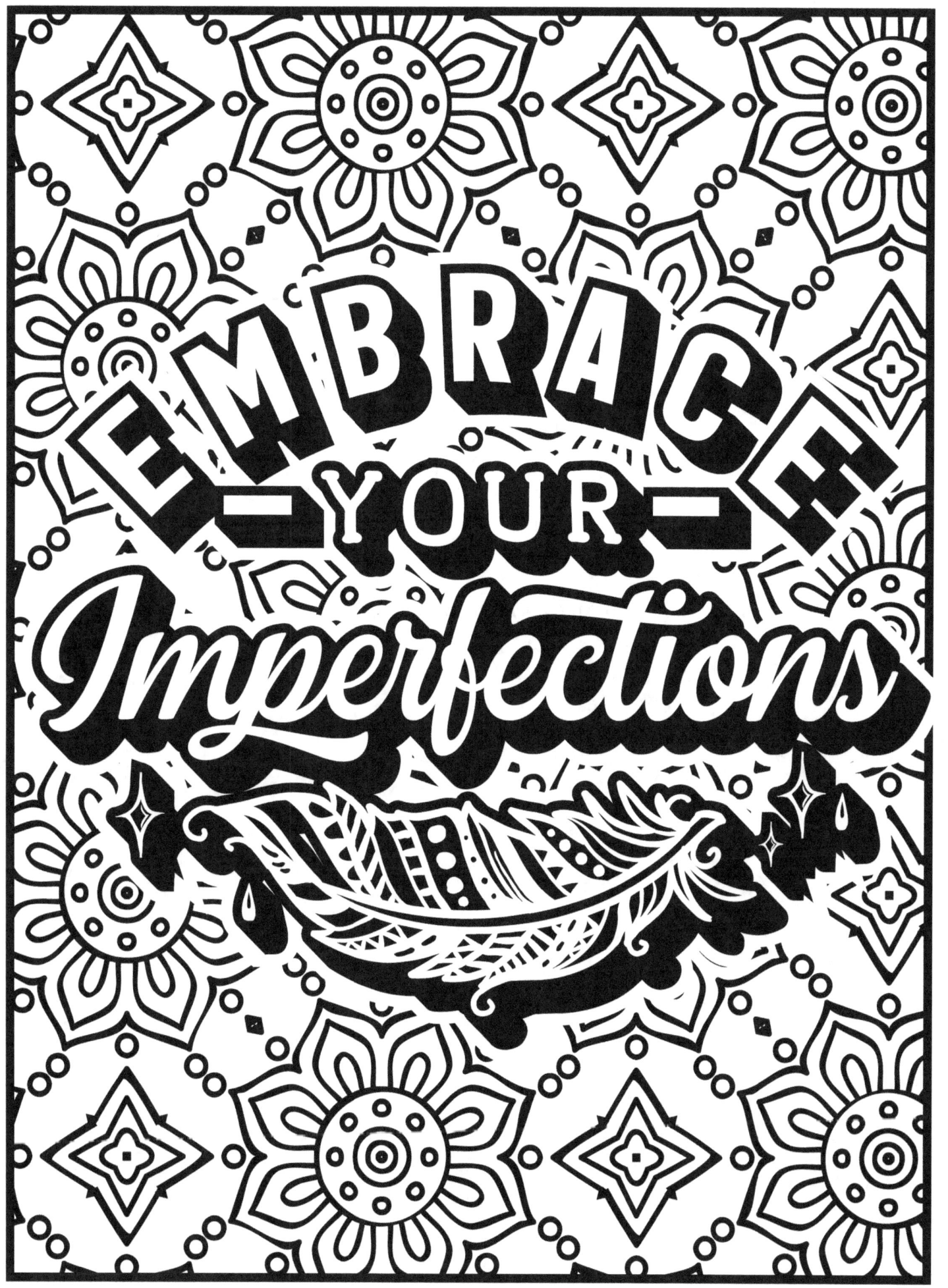

This page left intentionally blank.

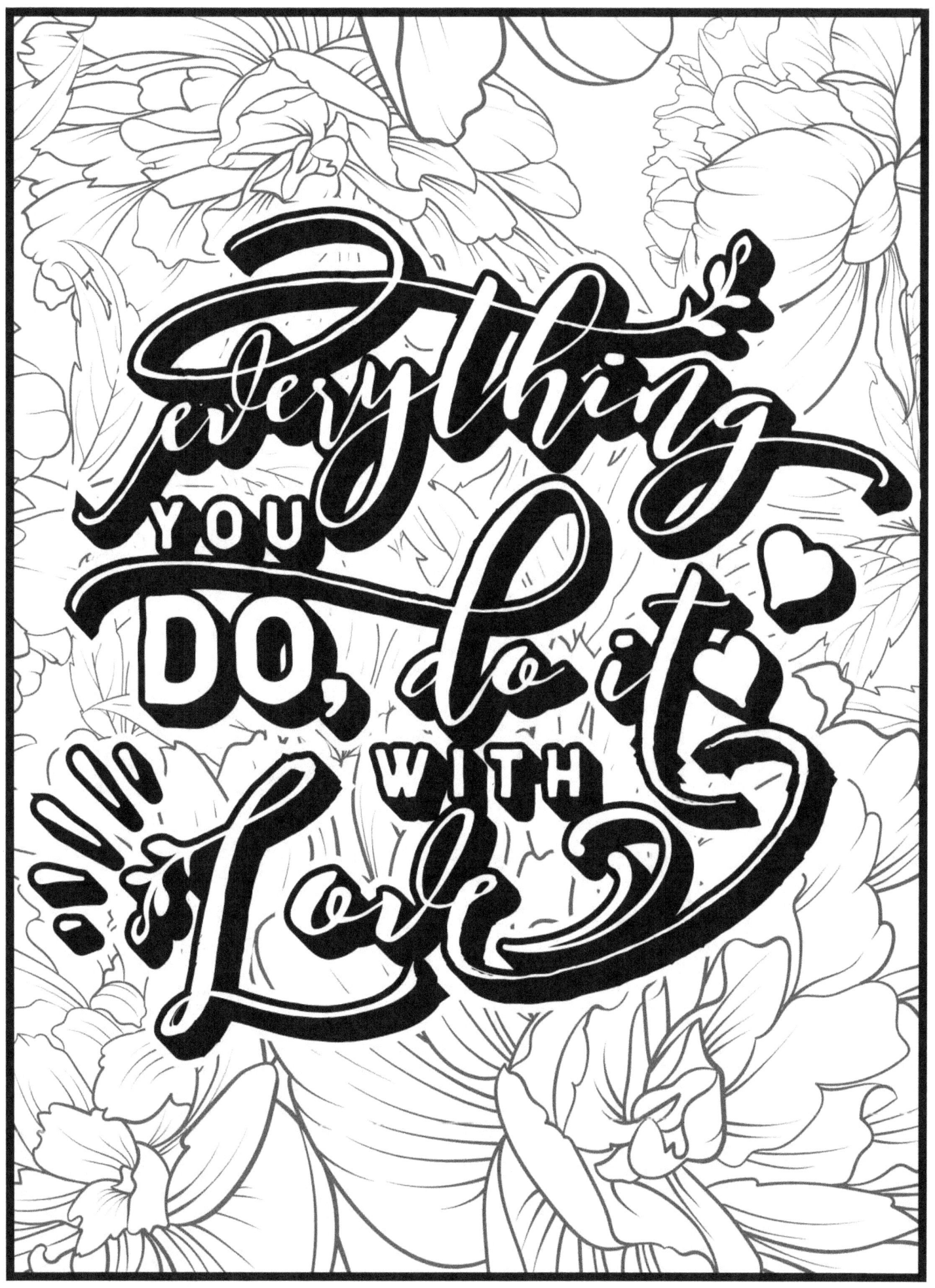

This page left intentionally blank.

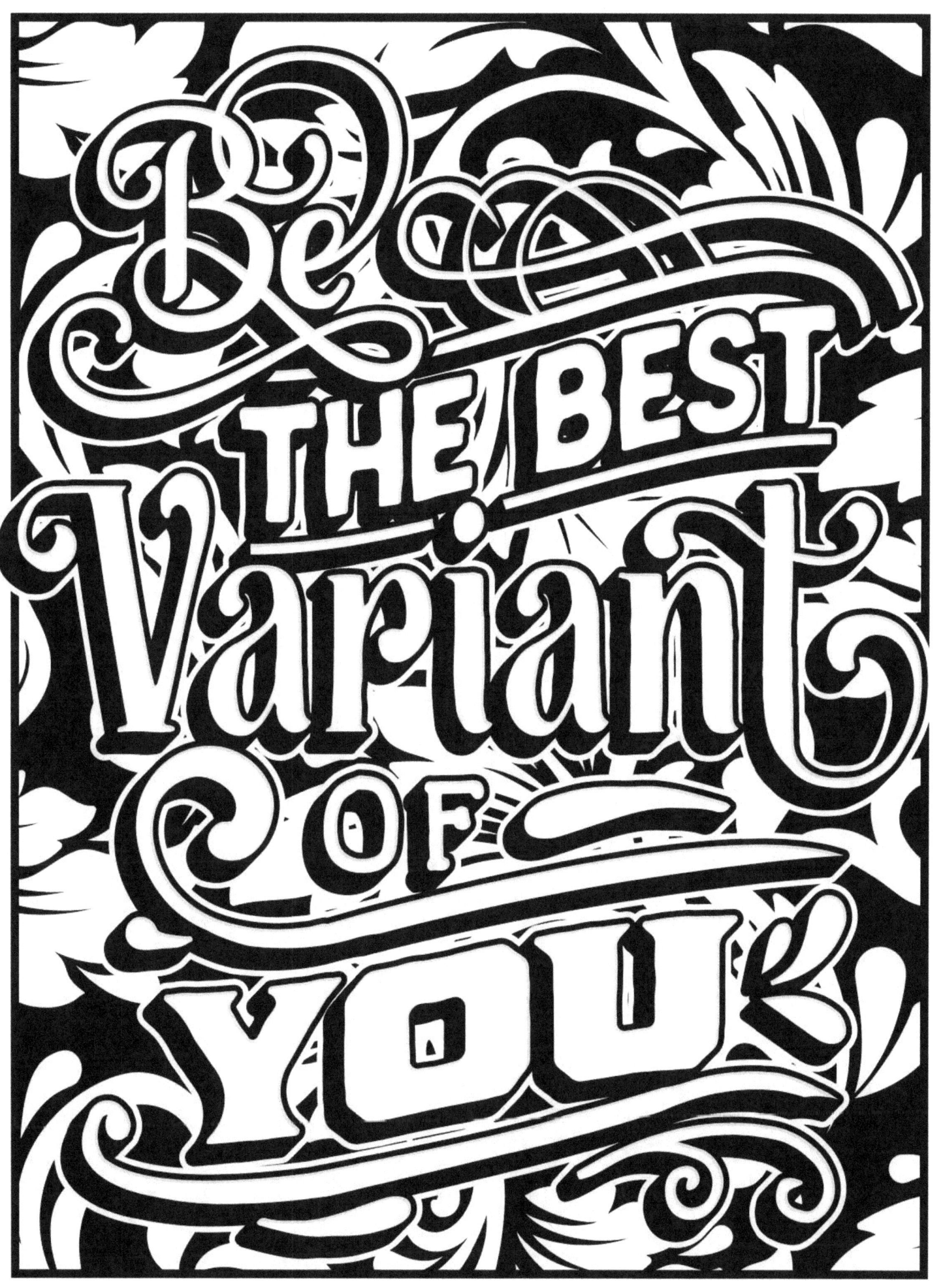

This page left intentionally blank.

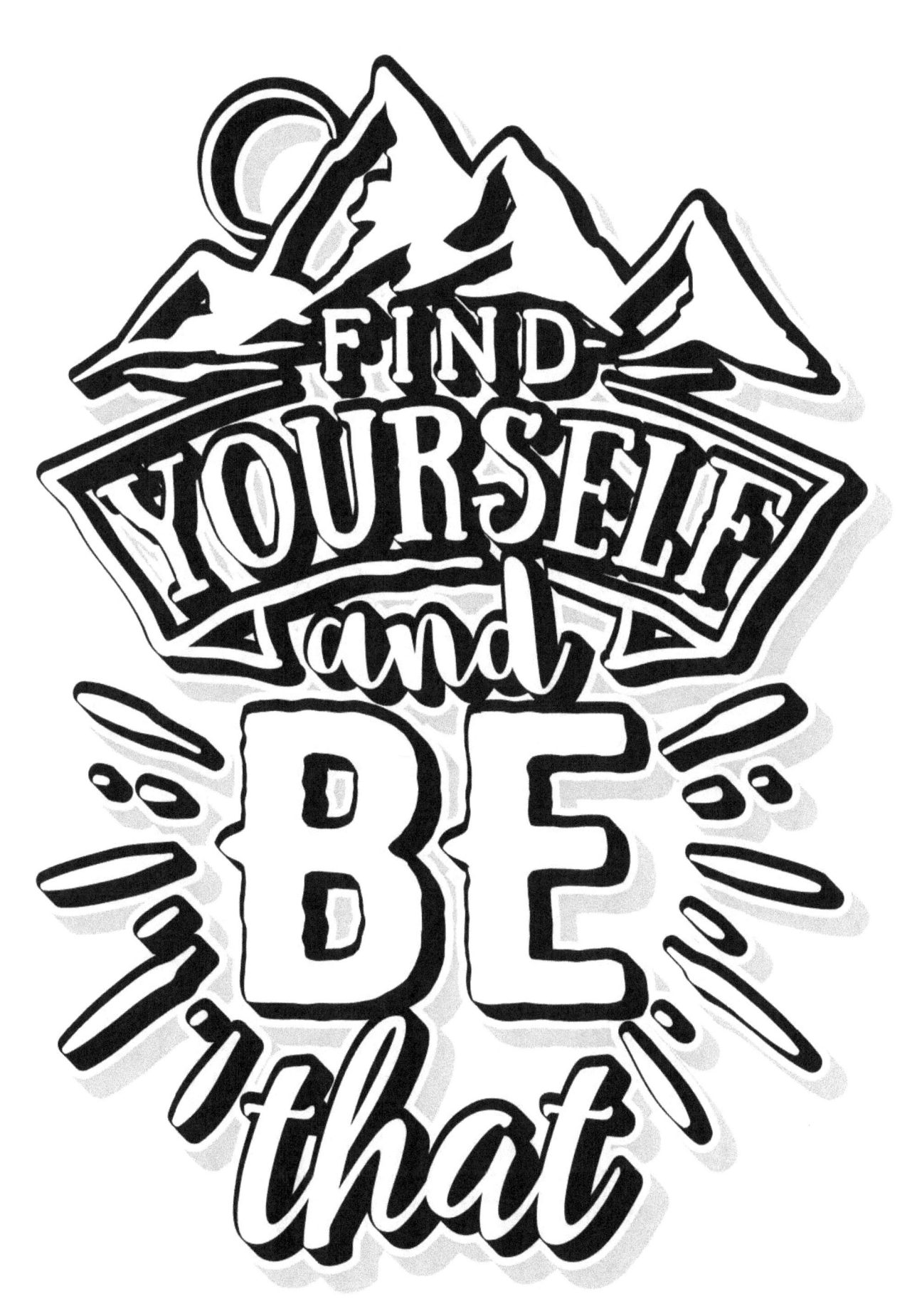

This page left intentionally blank.

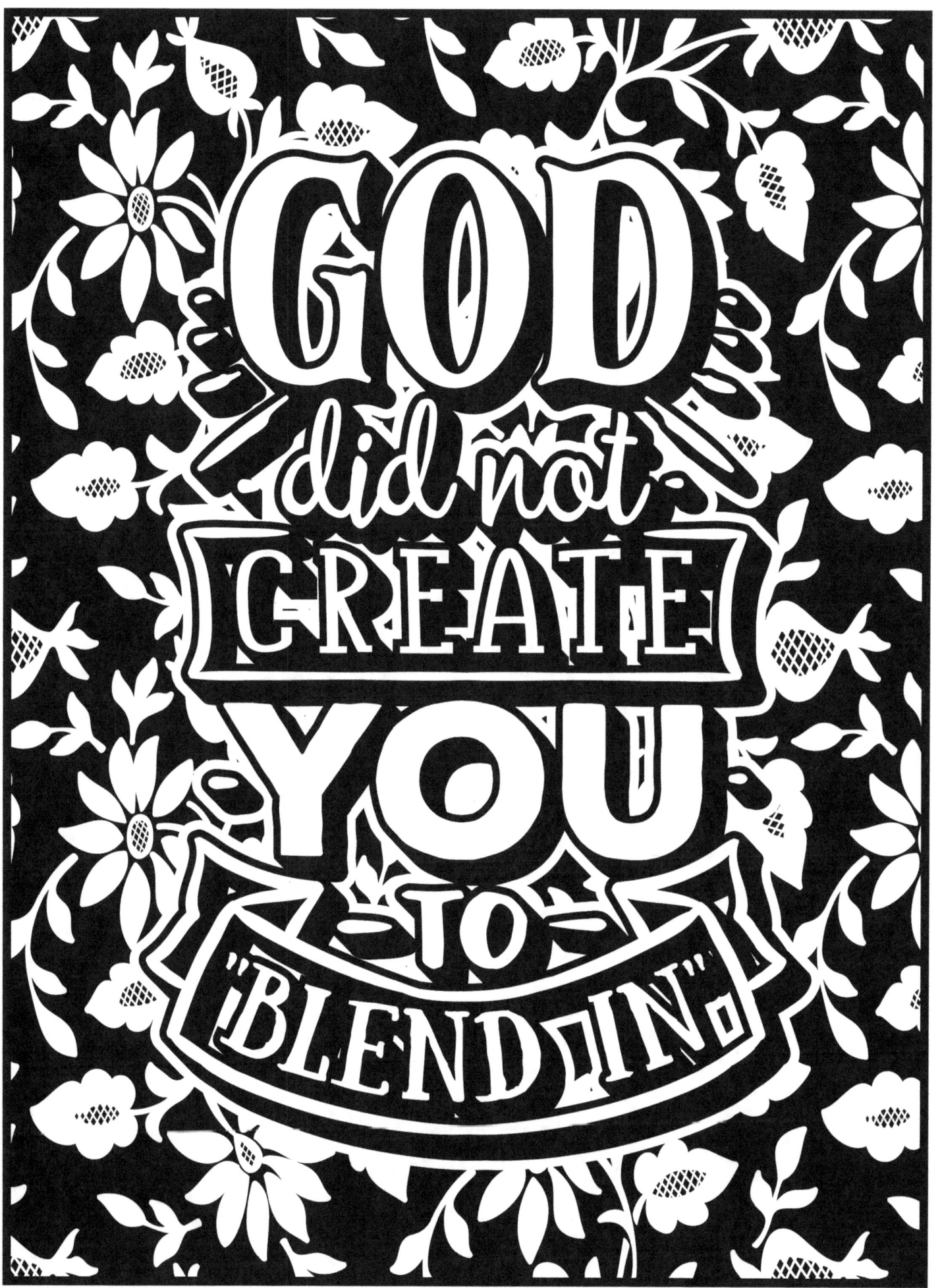

This page left intentionally blank.

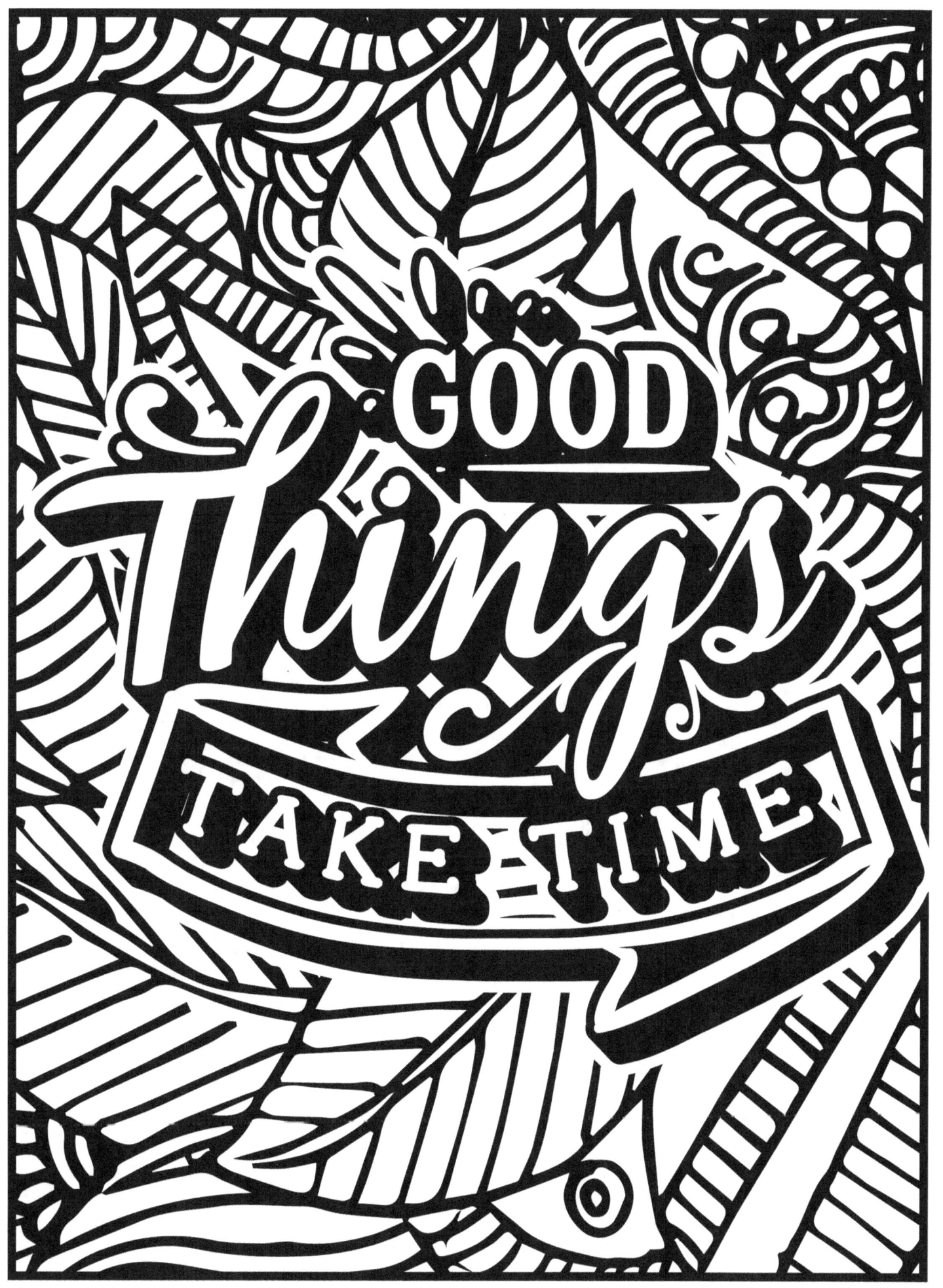

This page left intentionally blank.

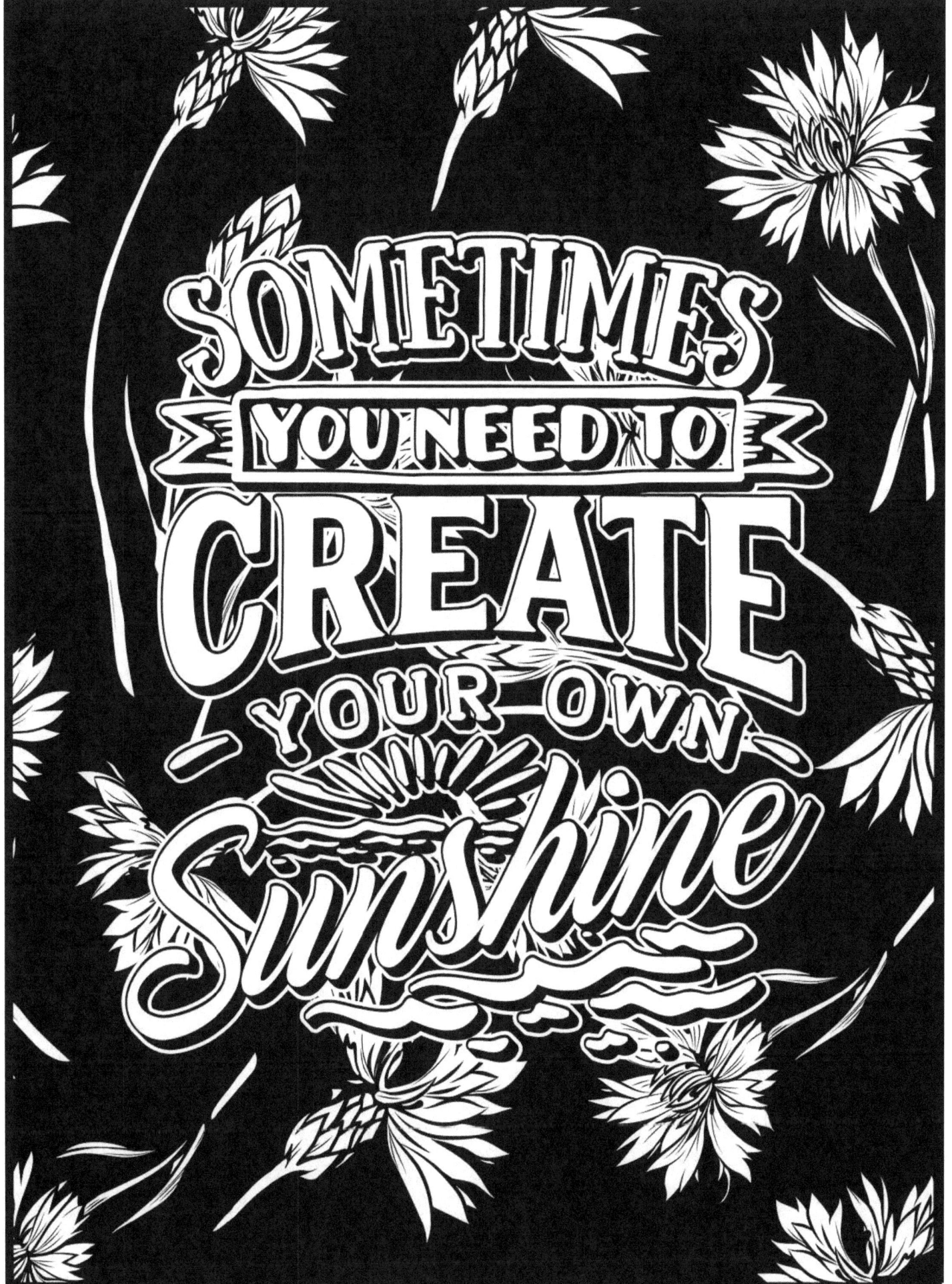

This page left intentionally blank.

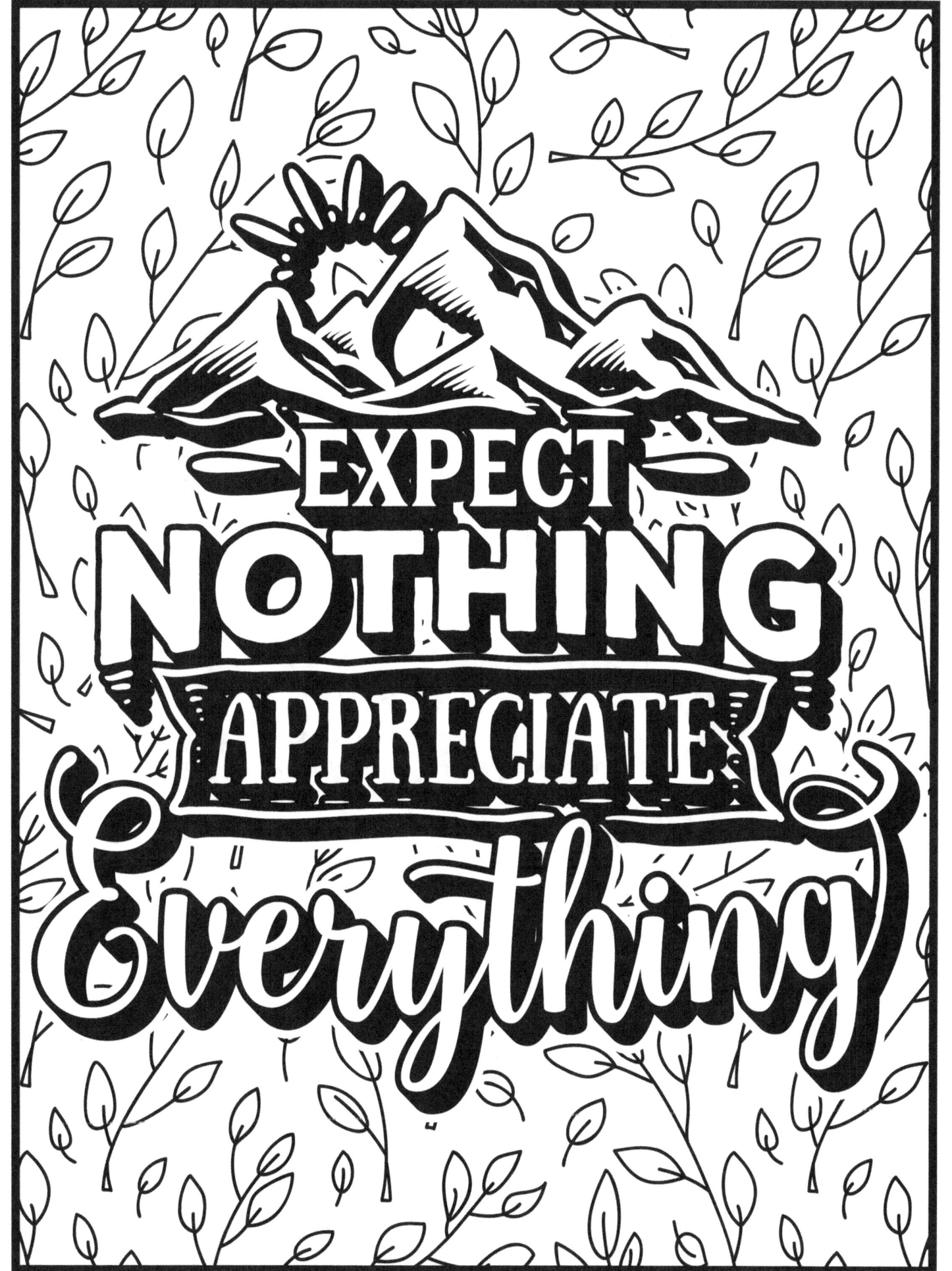

This page left intentionally blank.

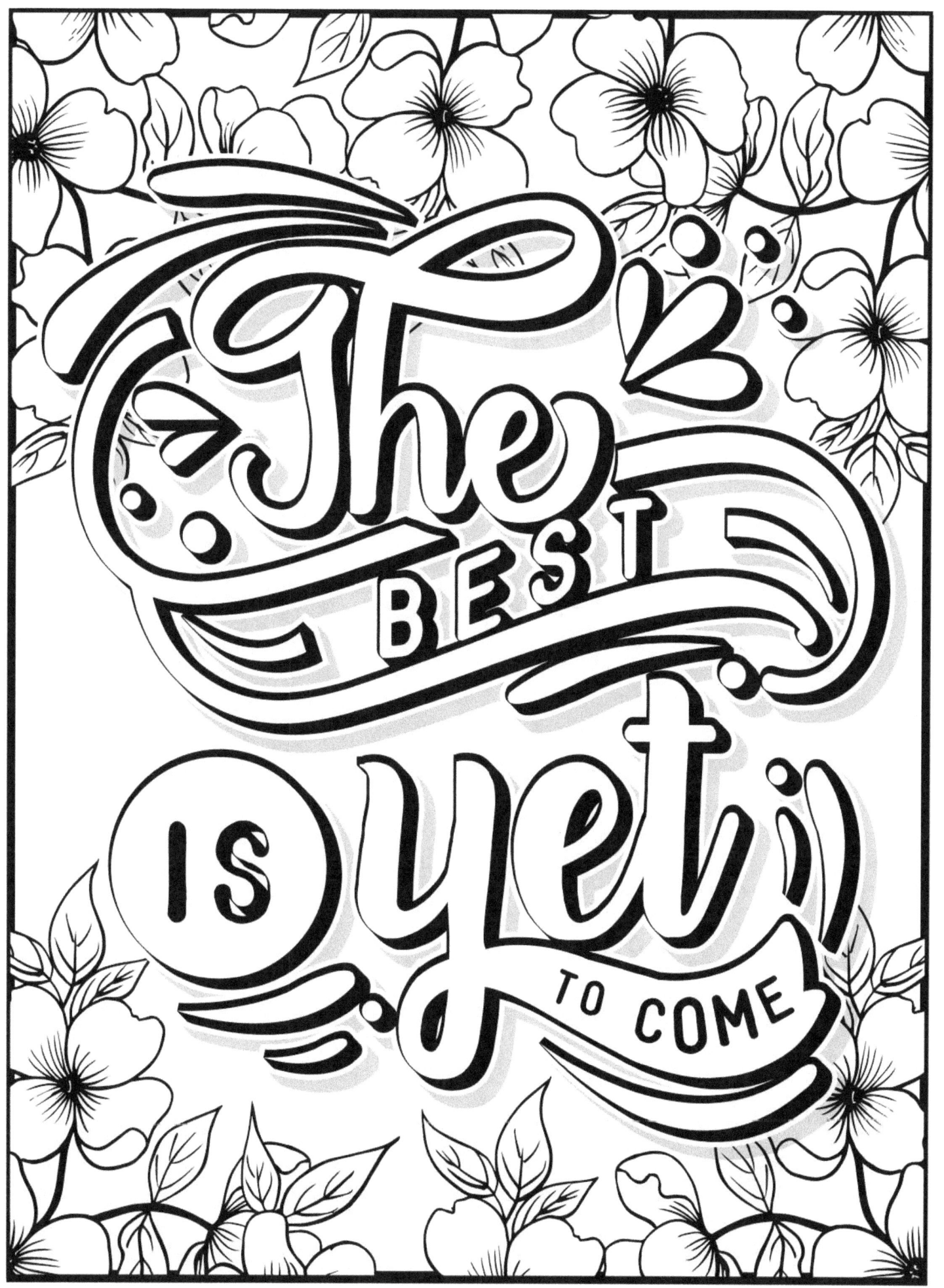

This page left intentionally blank.

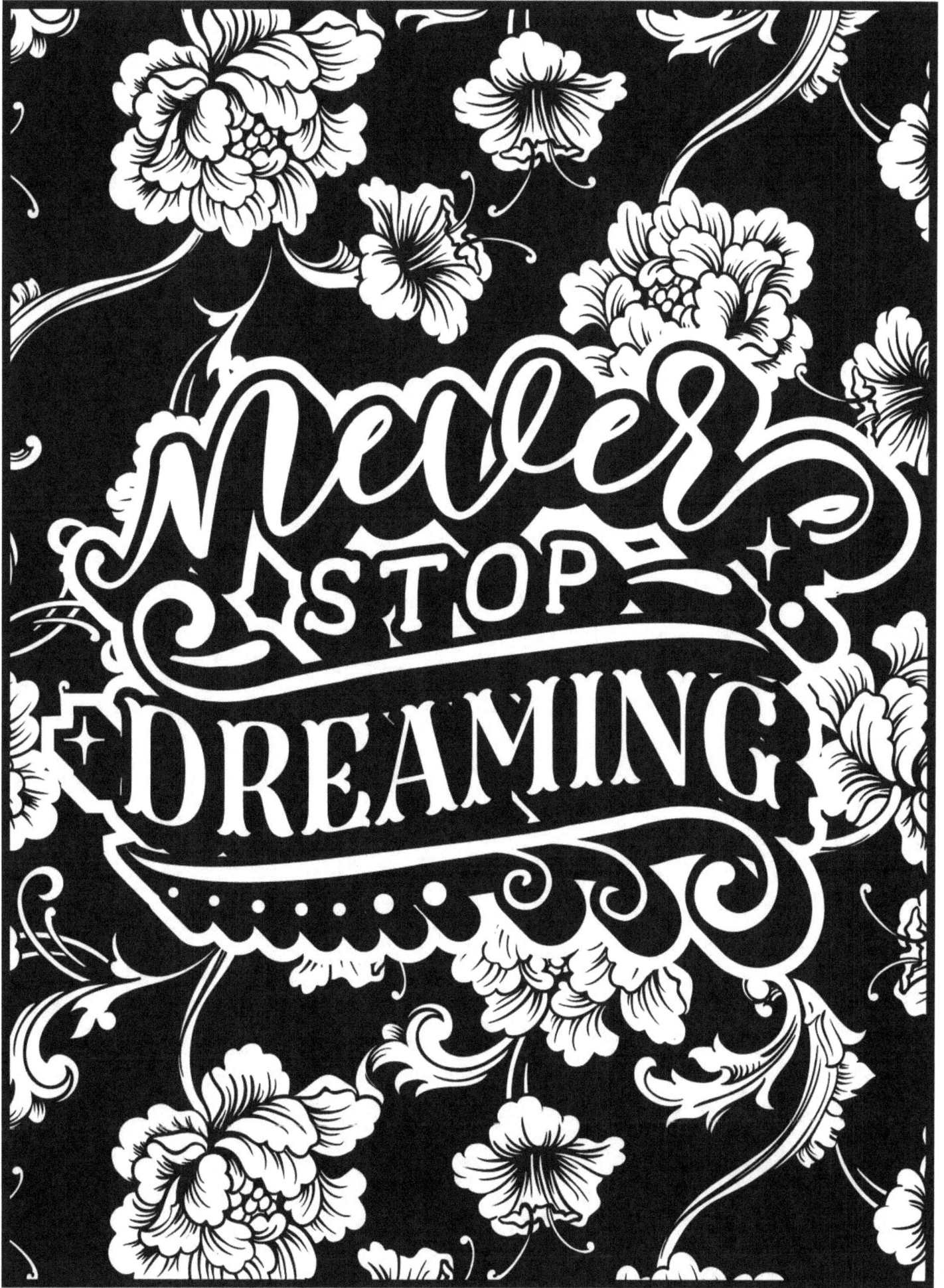

This page left intentionally blank.

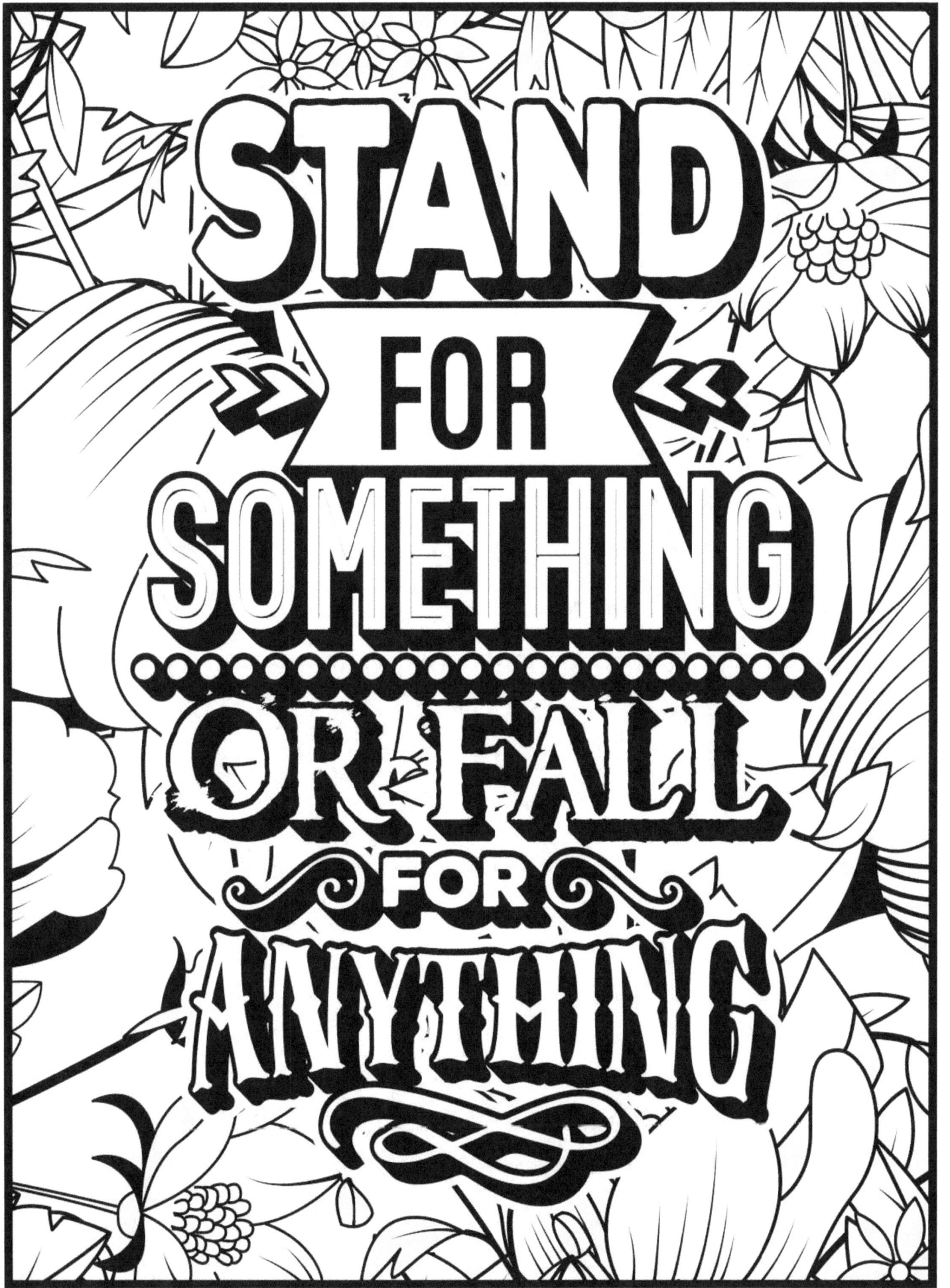

This page left intentionally blank.

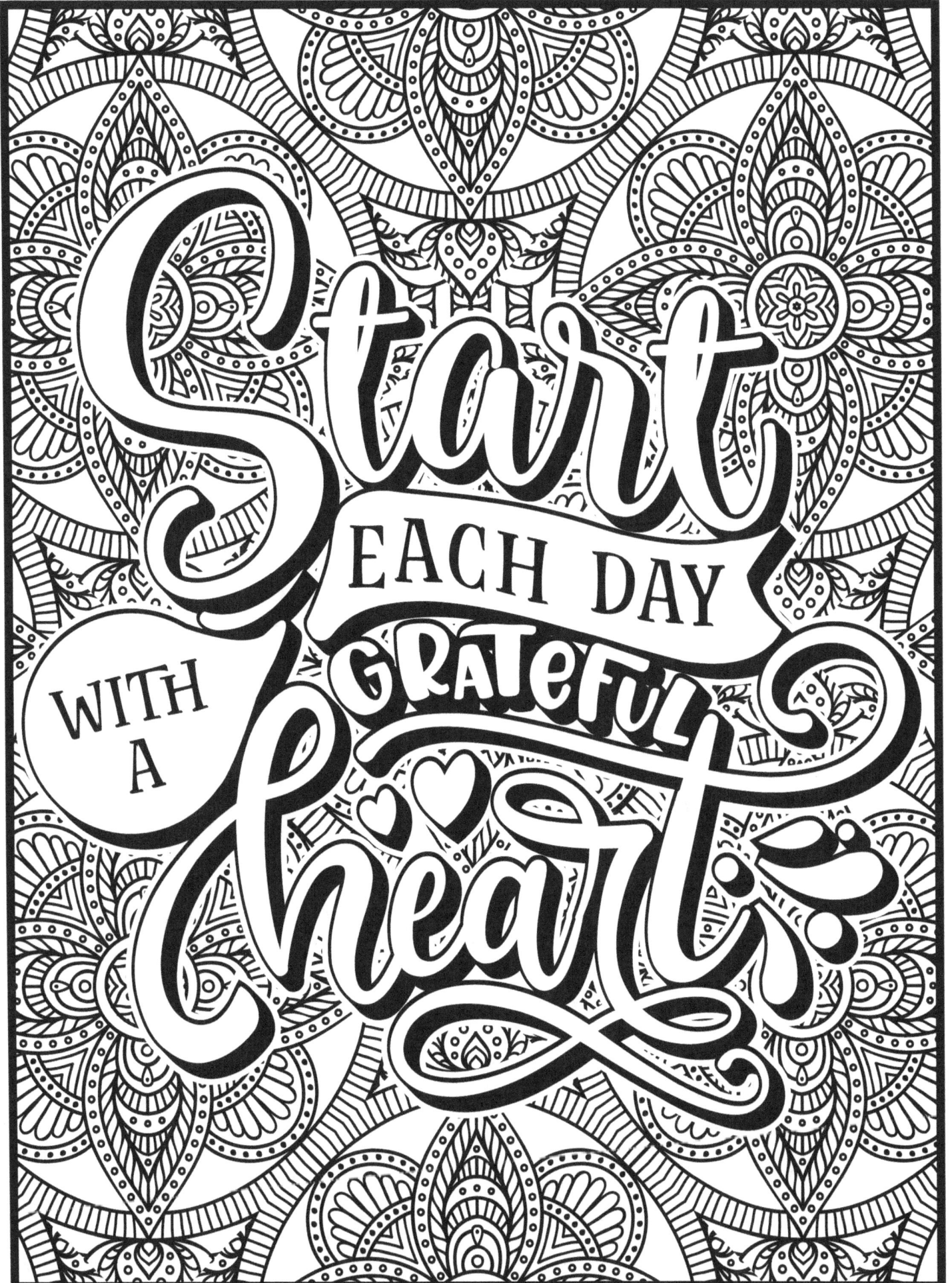

This page left intentionally blank.

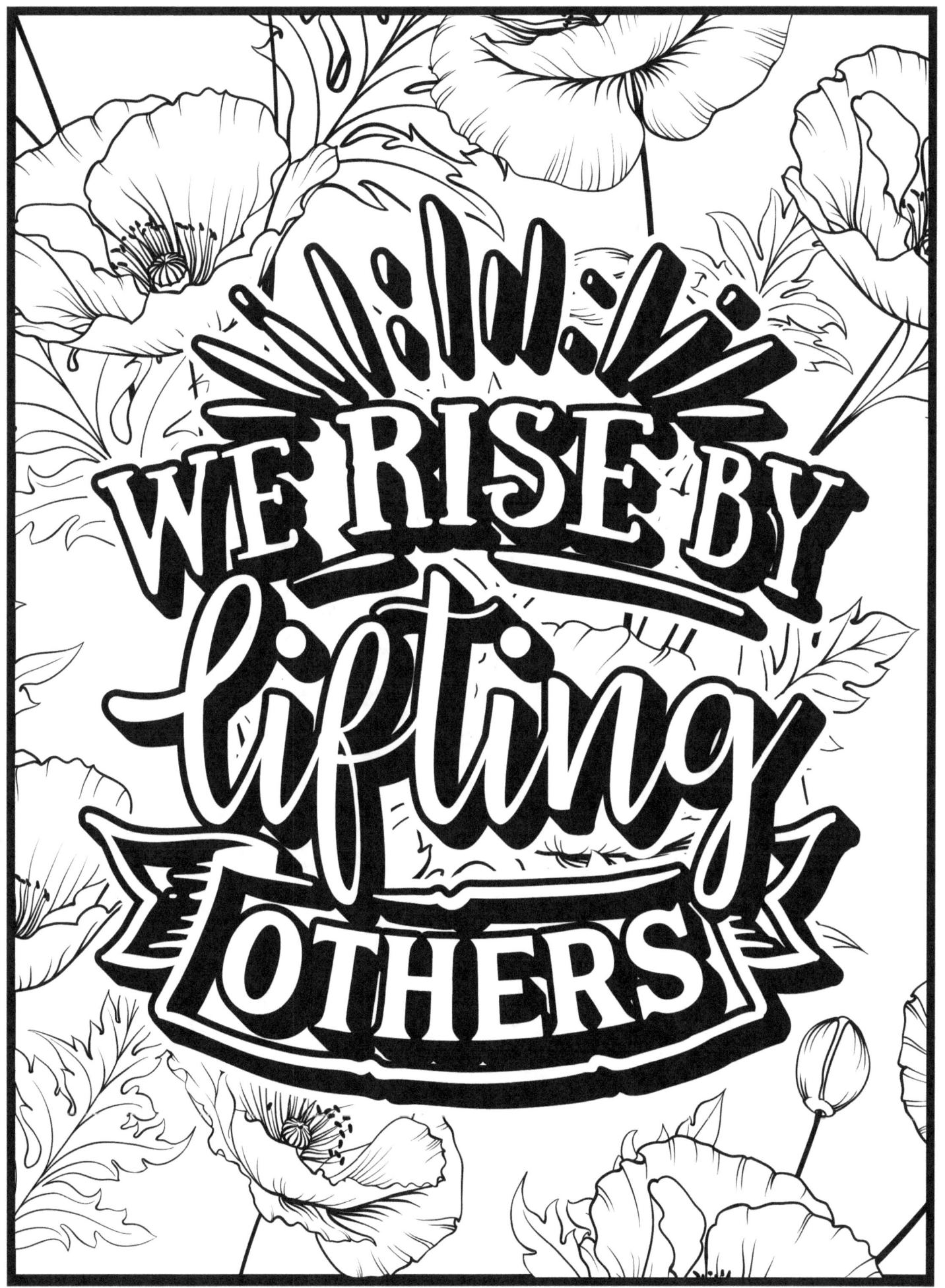

This page left intentionally blank.

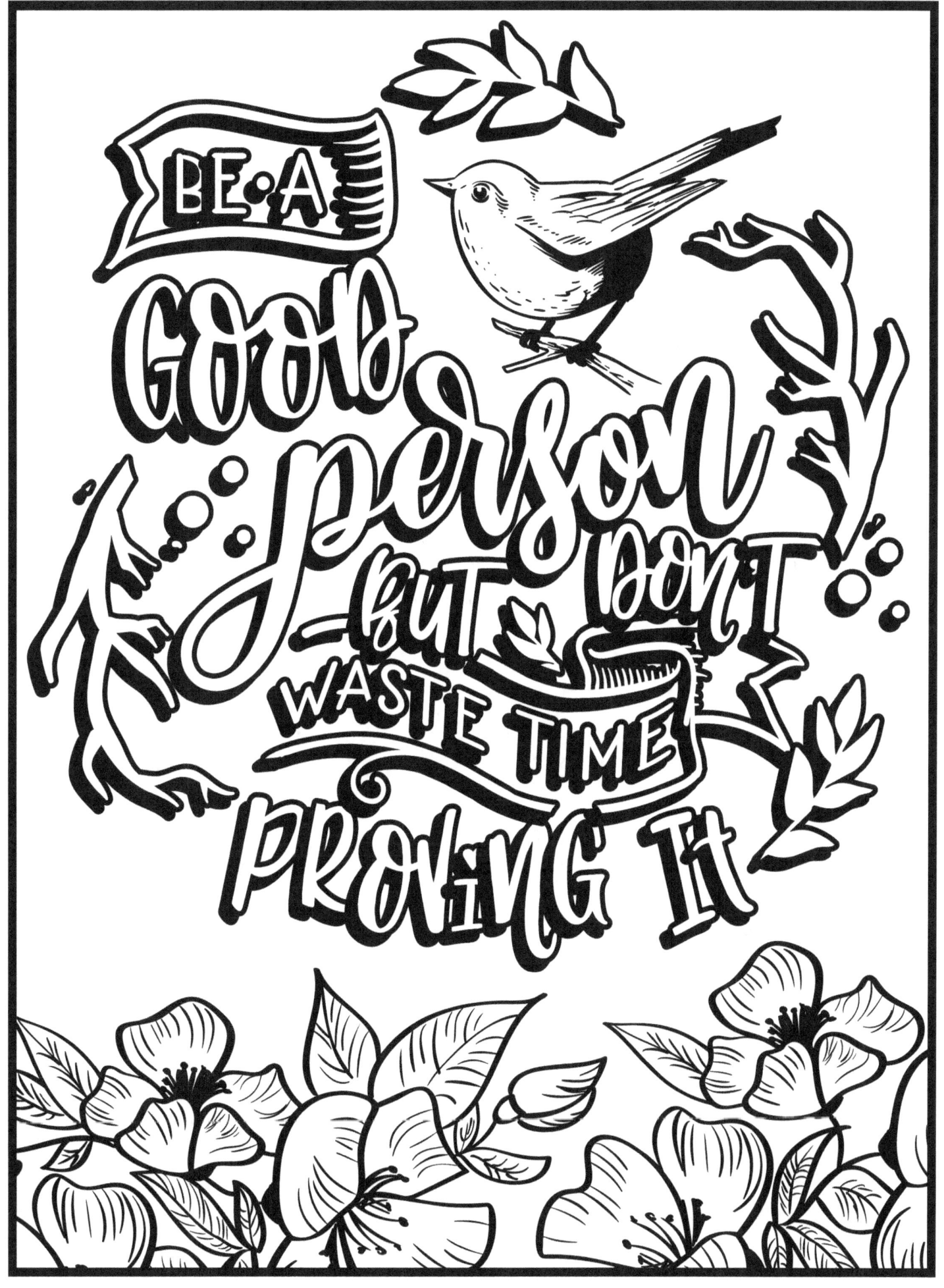

This page left intentionally blank.

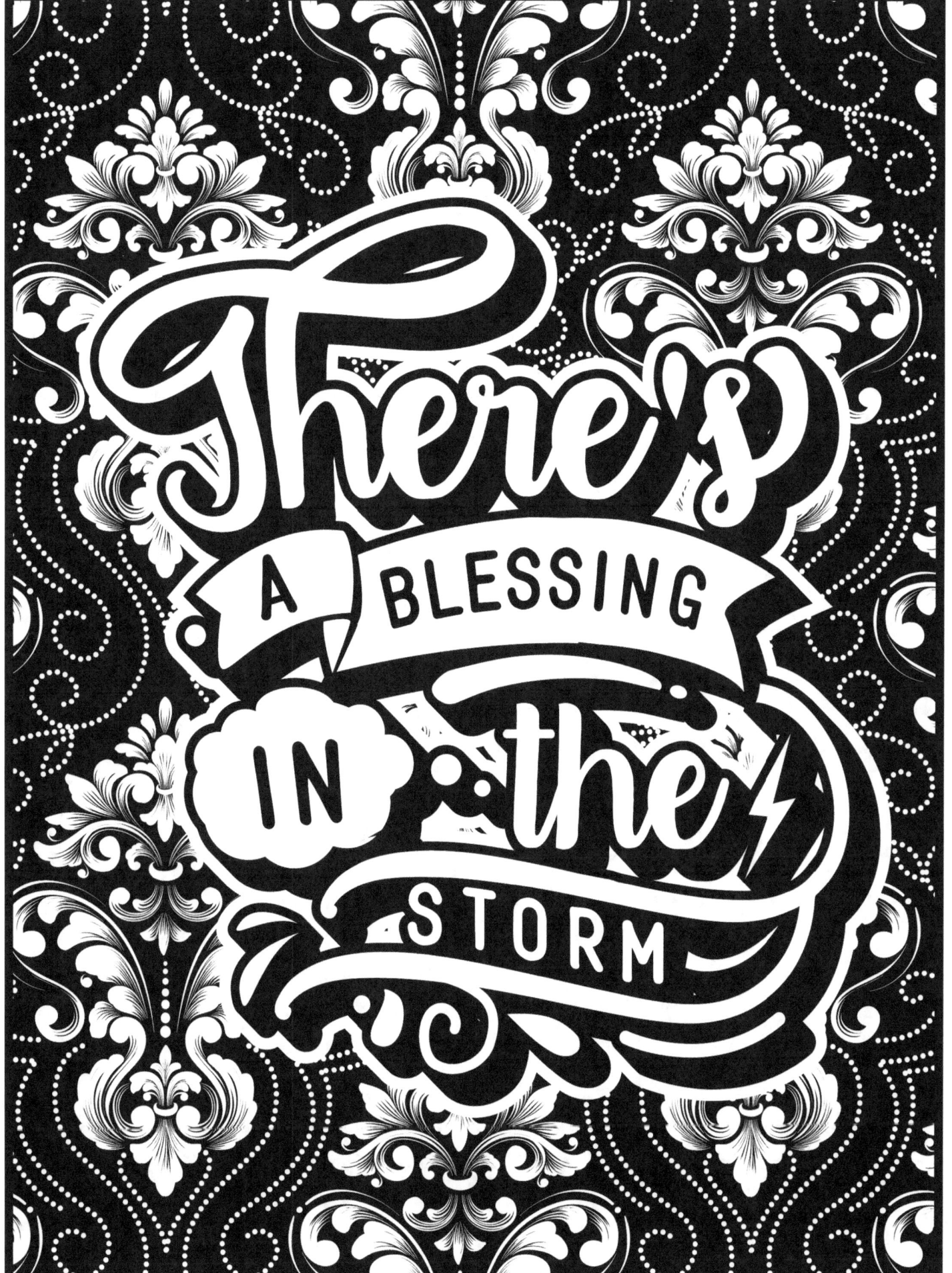

This page left intentionally blank.

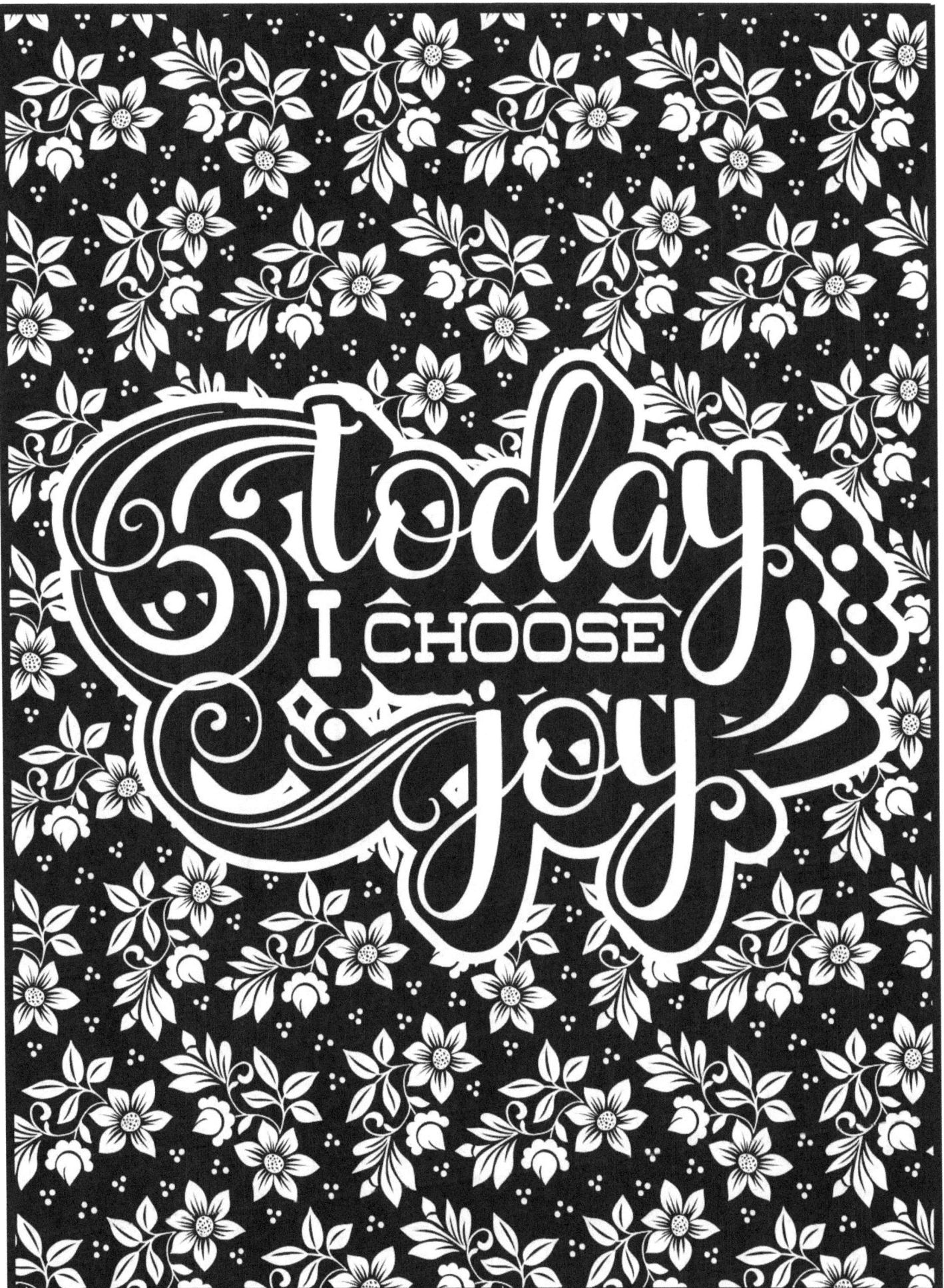

This page left intentionally blank.

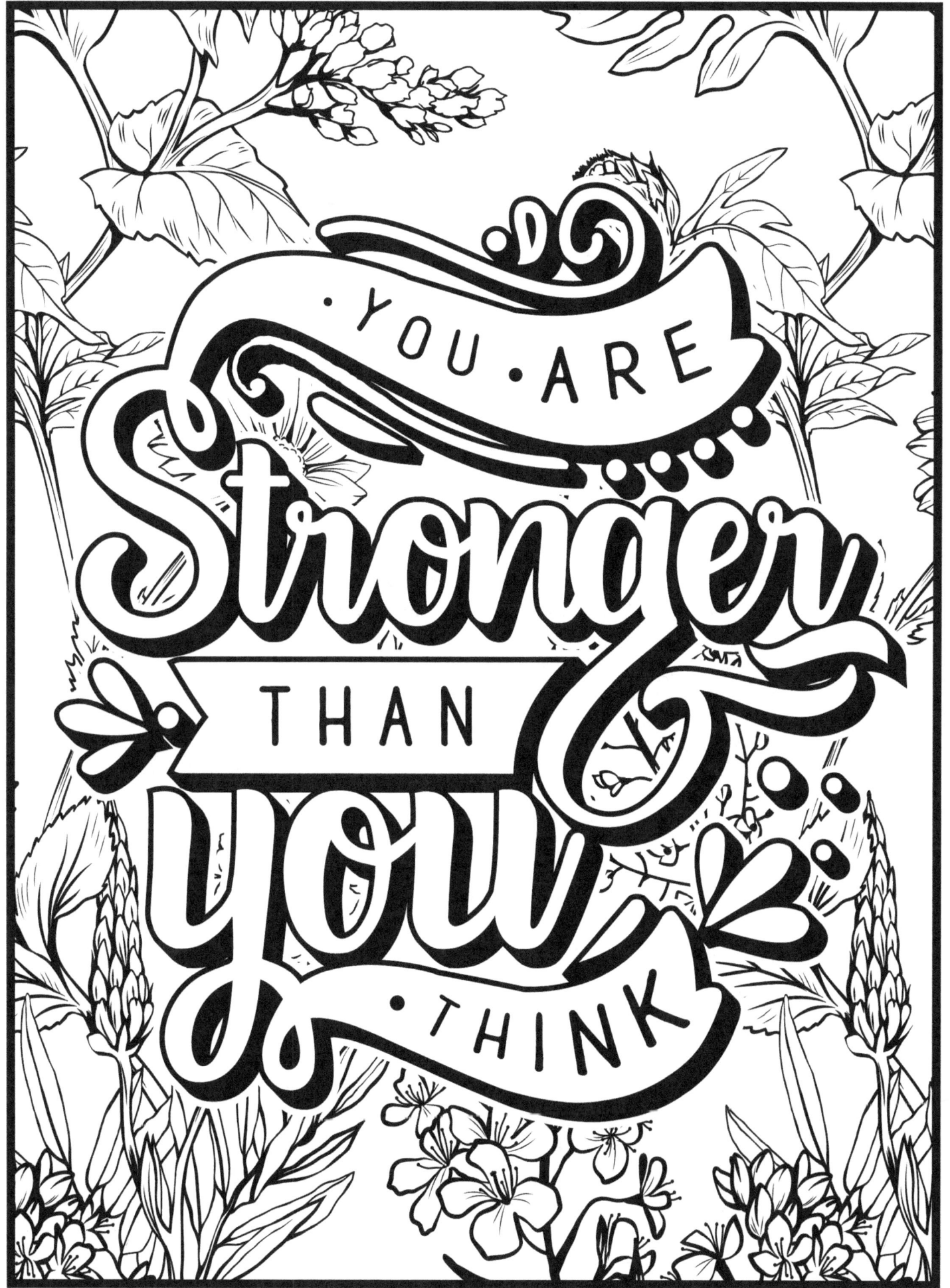

This page left intentionally blank.

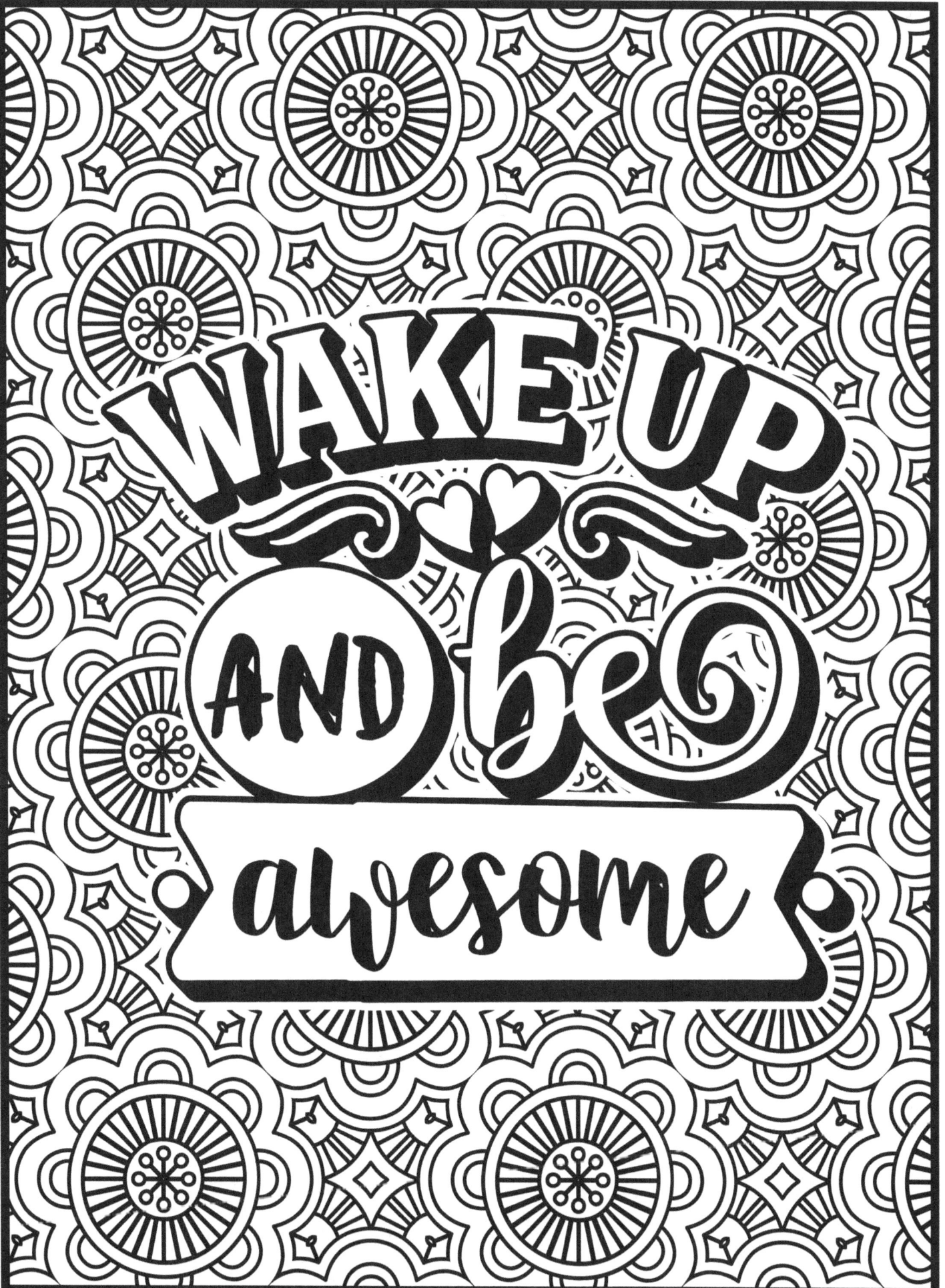

This page left intentionally blank.

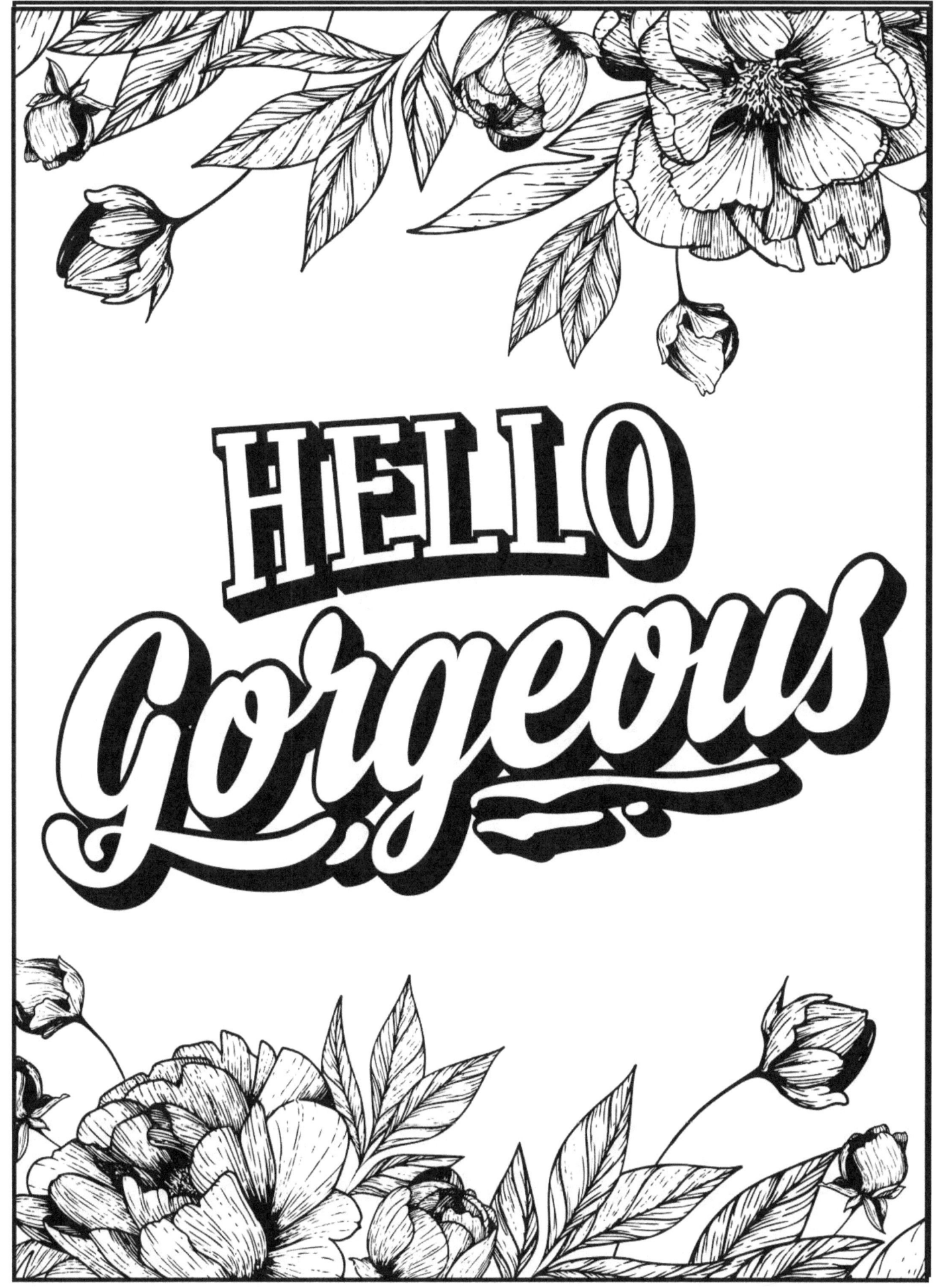

This page left intentionally blank.

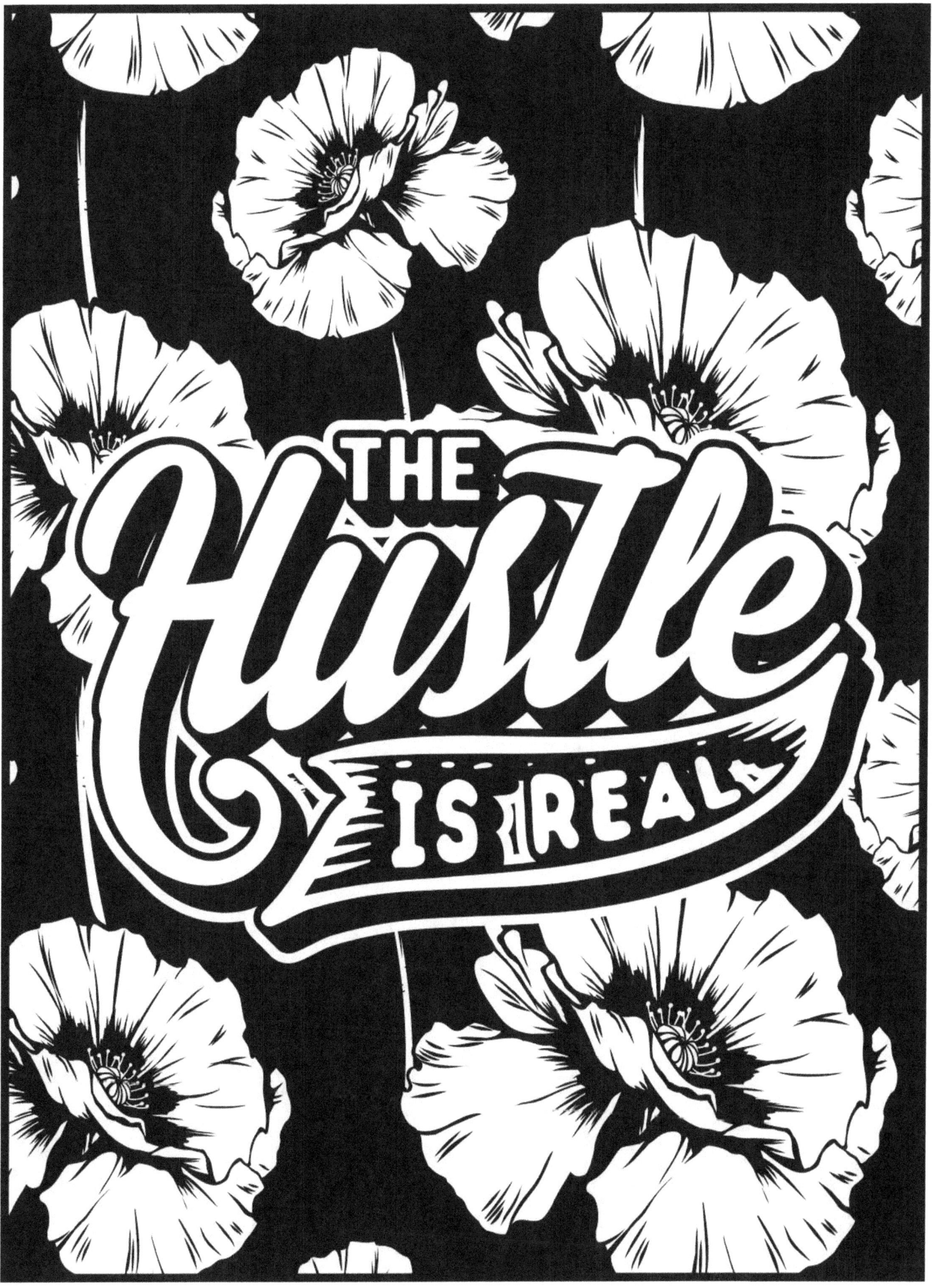

This page left intentionally blank.

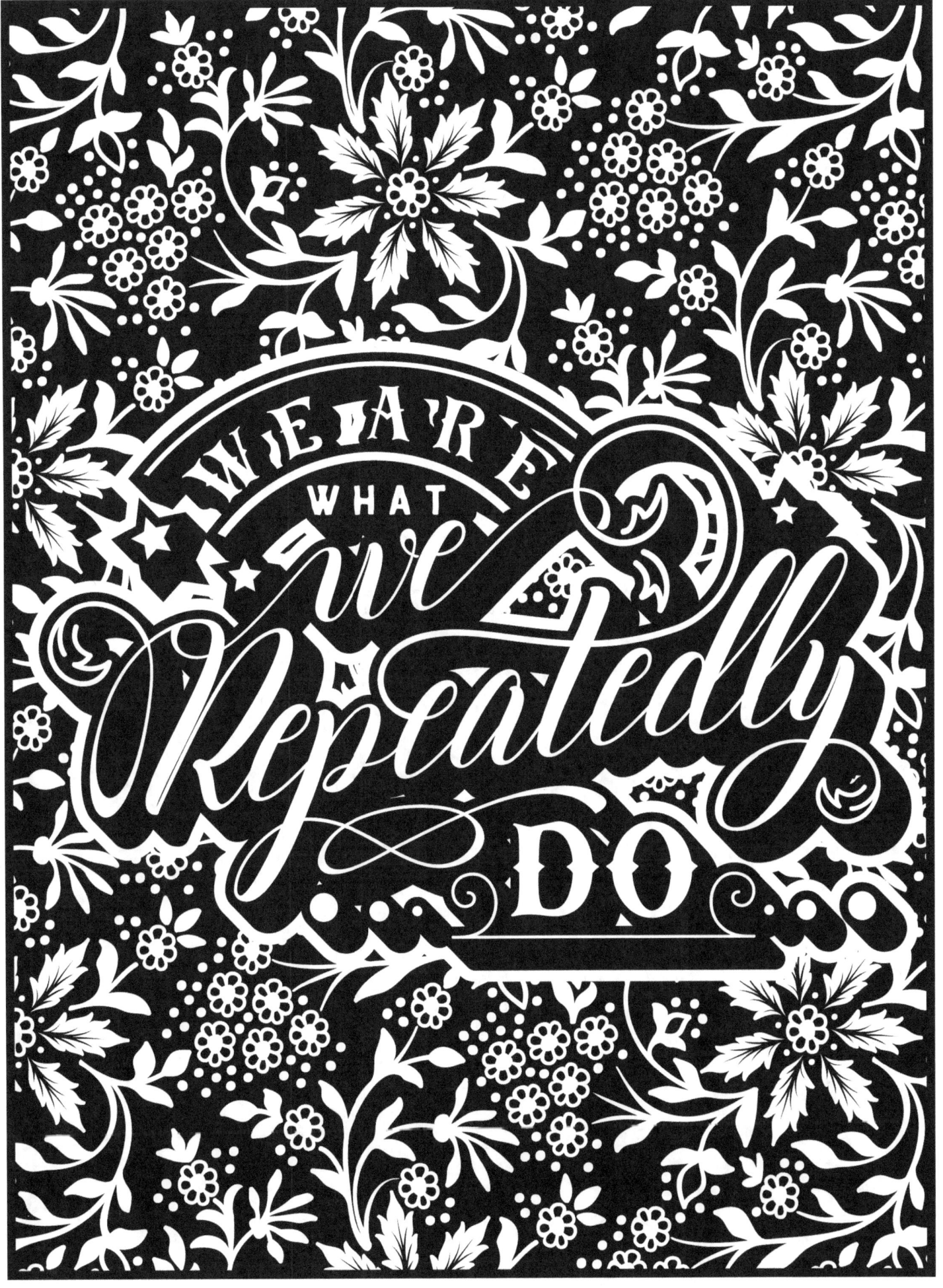

This page left intentionally blank.

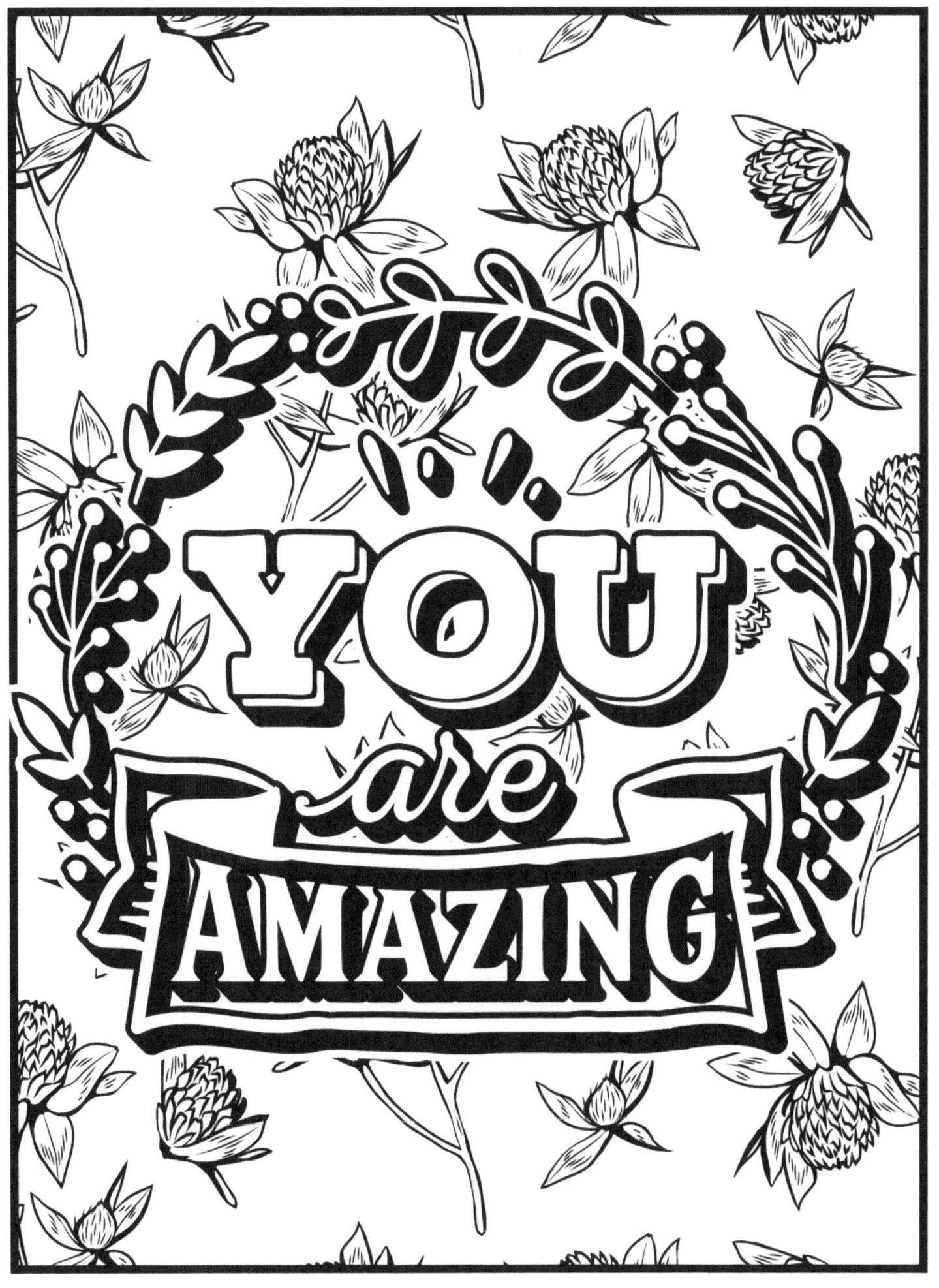

This page left intentionally blank.

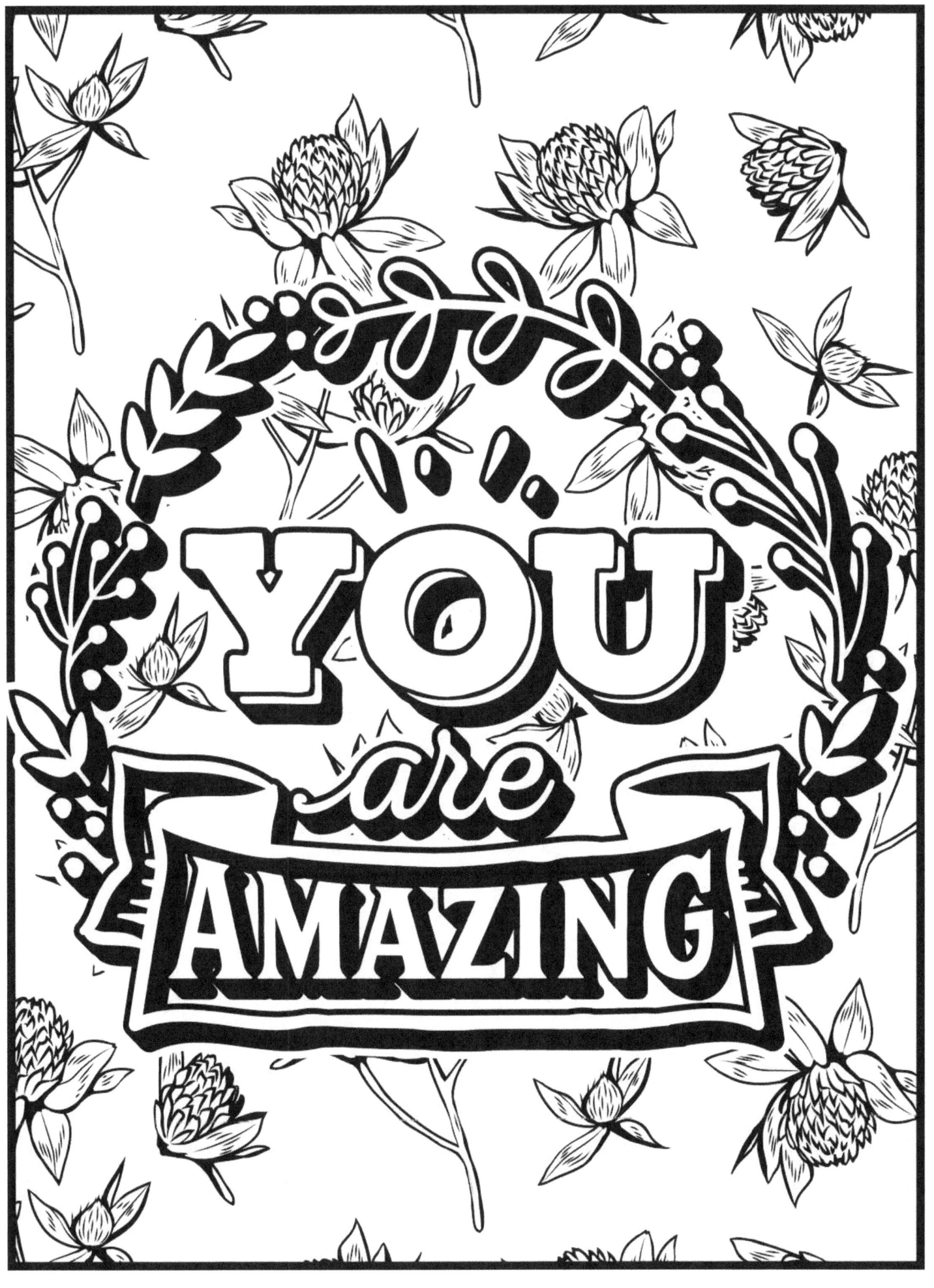

This page left intentionally blank.

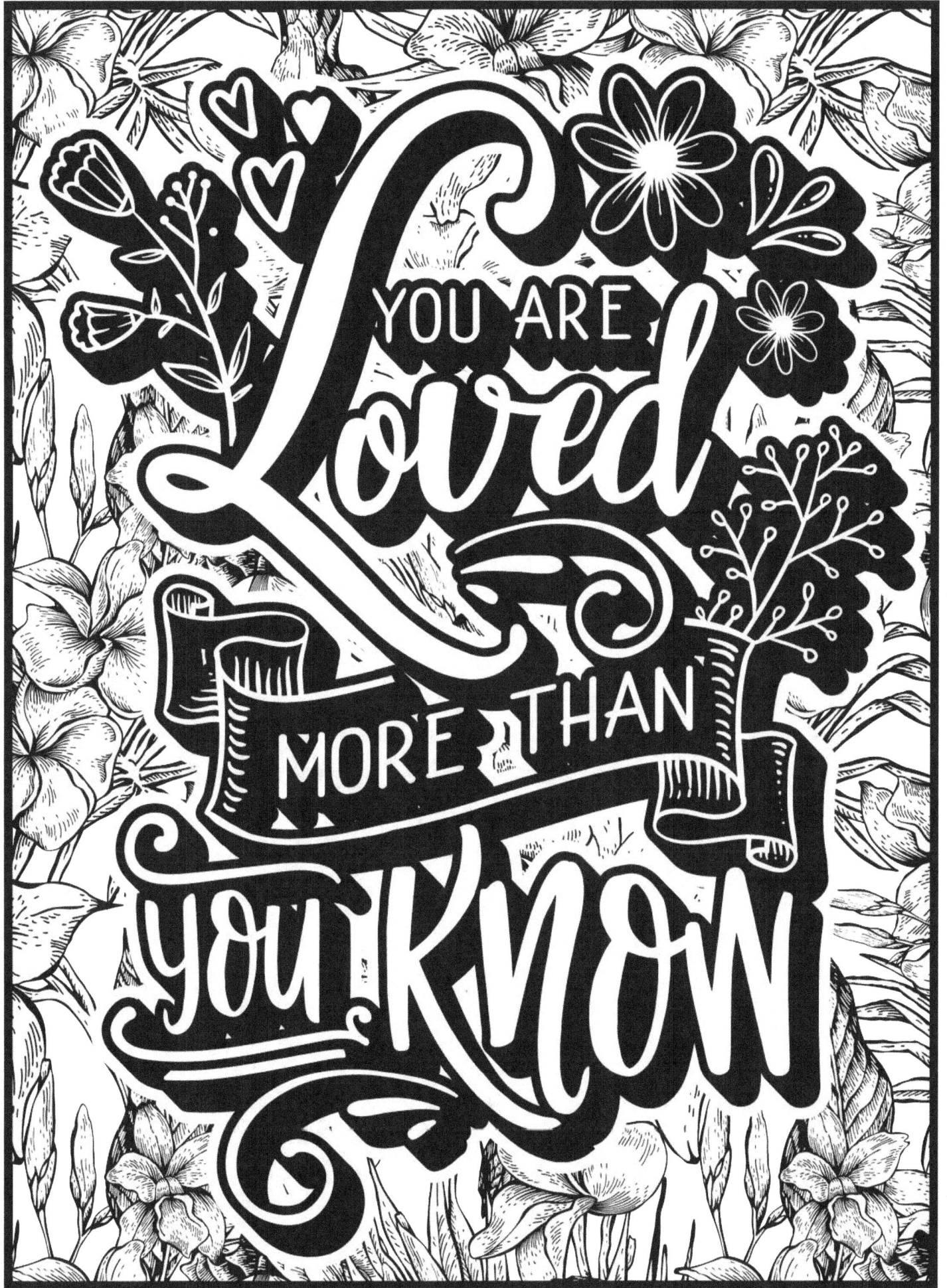

www.ingramcontent.com/pod-product-compliance
Lightning Source LLC
Chambersburg PA
CBHW082019230526
45466CB00022B/2691